W9-BZR-663

DATE DUE

| | | | |
|---|---|---|---|
| | | | |
| | | | |
| | | | |
| | | | |
| | | | |
| | | | |
| | | | |
| | | | |
| | | | |
| | | | |
| | | | |
| | | | |
| | | | |

# Science Projects and Activities

by Helen J. Challand, Ph.D.

illustrations by Linda Hoffman Kimball

 CHILDRENS PRESS ™

CHICAGO

Library of Congress Cataloging in Publication Data

Challand, Helen J.
  Science projects and activities.

  Includes index.
  Summary: Gives instructions for science projects and
experiments involving an ant colony, a chicken brooder, plant
grafting, microphotography, water purification, and other
topics.
  1. Science—Experiments—Juvenile literature.
[1. Science—Experiments. 2. Experiments] I. Title.
Q163.C36  1985      507′.8      84-23252
ISBN 0-516-00569-3

        8 9 10 R 94 93 92 91 90 89

# TABLE OF CONTENTS

Animal Houses . . . . . . . . . . . . . . . . . . . . . . . . . . . . . . . . . . . . . . . . . . . . . . .9
Animal Tracks . . . . . . . . . . . . . . . . . . . . . . . . . . . . . . . . . . . . . . . . . . . . . . .10
Ant Colony . . . . . . . . . . . . . . . . . . . . . . . . . . . . . . . . . . . . . . . . . . . . . . . . . .10
Aquarium Projection . . . . . . . . . . . . . . . . . . . . . . . . . . . . . . . . . . . . . . . . .11
Arachnids . . . . . . . . . . . . . . . . . . . . . . . . . . . . . . . . . . . . . . . . . . . . . . . . . . .12
Balance Scale . . . . . . . . . . . . . . . . . . . . . . . . . . . . . . . . . . . . . . . . . . . . . . .12
Ball Bearings . . . . . . . . . . . . . . . . . . . . . . . . . . . . . . . . . . . . . . . . . . . . . . . .13
Belt-Driven Machines . . . . . . . . . . . . . . . . . . . . . . . . . . . . . . . . . . . . . . . .14
Birdhouses . . . . . . . . . . . . . . . . . . . . . . . . . . . . . . . . . . . . . . . . . . . . . . . . .14
Blueprinting . . . . . . . . . . . . . . . . . . . . . . . . . . . . . . . . . . . . . . . . . . . . . . . .16
Bone and Muscle Model . . . . . . . . . . . . . . . . . . . . . . . . . . . . . . . . . . . . .16
Burner Using Alcohol . . . . . . . . . . . . . . . . . . . . . . . . . . . . . . . . . . . . . . .18
Camera . . . . . . . . . . . . . . . . . . . . . . . . . . . . . . . . . . . . . . . . . . . . . . . . . . . .18
Caterpillars . . . . . . . . . . . . . . . . . . . . . . . . . . . . . . . . . . . . . . . . . . . . . . . .19
Cell Models . . . . . . . . . . . . . . . . . . . . . . . . . . . . . . . . . . . . . . . . . . . . . . . .20
Charts . . . . . . . . . . . . . . . . . . . . . . . . . . . . . . . . . . . . . . . . . . . . . . . . . . . . .20
Chicken Brooder . . . . . . . . . . . . . . . . . . . . . . . . . . . . . . . . . . . . . . . . . . .21
Chromatography . . . . . . . . . . . . . . . . . . . . . . . . . . . . . . . . . . . . . . . . . . . .22
Circulation . . . . . . . . . . . . . . . . . . . . . . . . . . . . . . . . . . . . . . . . . . . . . . . . .23
Compass Travels . . . . . . . . . . . . . . . . . . . . . . . . . . . . . . . . . . . . . . . . . . . .24
Compost Pile . . . . . . . . . . . . . . . . . . . . . . . . . . . . . . . . . . . . . . . . . . . . . . .25
Compound Machines . . . . . . . . . . . . . . . . . . . . . . . . . . . . . . . . . . . . . . . .26
Diazo Paper Prints . . . . . . . . . . . . . . . . . . . . . . . . . . . . . . . . . . . . . . . . . .27
Eclipse Viewer . . . . . . . . . . . . . . . . . . . . . . . . . . . . . . . . . . . . . . . . . . . . . .28
Electric Quiz Game . . . . . . . . . . . . . . . . . . . . . . . . . . . . . . . . . . . . . . . . .28
Electrical Switch . . . . . . . . . . . . . . . . . . . . . . . . . . . . . . . . . . . . . . . . . . . .30
Electromagnet . . . . . . . . . . . . . . . . . . . . . . . . . . . . . . . . . . . . . . . . . . . . . .30
Electroscope . . . . . . . . . . . . . . . . . . . . . . . . . . . . . . . . . . . . . . . . . . . . . . .31
Elements . . . . . . . . . . . . . . . . . . . . . . . . . . . . . . . . . . . . . . . . . . . . . . . . . . .32
Embedding in Plastic . . . . . . . . . . . . . . . . . . . . . . . . . . . . . . . . . . . . . . . .34
Fern Cycle . . . . . . . . . . . . . . . . . . . . . . . . . . . . . . . . . . . . . . . . . . . . . . . . .35
Floral Diagrams . . . . . . . . . . . . . . . . . . . . . . . . . . . . . . . . . . . . . . . . . . . .36
Flower Preservation . . . . . . . . . . . . . . . . . . . . . . . . . . . . . . . . . . . . . . . . .37
Galvanometer . . . . . . . . . . . . . . . . . . . . . . . . . . . . . . . . . . . . . . . . . . . . . .38
Grafting Plants . . . . . . . . . . . . . . . . . . . . . . . . . . . . . . . . . . . . . . . . . . . . .38

Greenhouse . . . . . . . . . . . . . . . . . . . . . . . . . . . . . . . . . . . . . . . . . . . . . . . . . . . .39
Guinea Pigs . . . . . . . . . . . . . . . . . . . . . . . . . . . . . . . . . . . . . . . . . . . . . . . . . . .40
Guppies . . . . . . . . . . . . . . . . . . . . . . . . . . . . . . . . . . . . . . . . . . . . . . . . . . . . .40
Heart Inside and Out . . . . . . . . . . . . . . . . . . . . . . . . . . . . . . . . . . . . . . . . .41
Herb Garden . . . . . . . . . . . . . . . . . . . . . . . . . . . . . . . . . . . . . . . . . . . . . . . . .42
Heredity . . . . . . . . . . . . . . . . . . . . . . . . . . . . . . . . . . . . . . . . . . . . . . . . . . . . .42
Hibernation of Frogs . . . . . . . . . . . . . . . . . . . . . . . . . . . . . . . . . . . . . . . . .44
Hydrometer . . . . . . . . . . . . . . . . . . . . . . . . . . . . . . . . . . . . . . . . . . . . . . . . . .44
Incubator . . . . . . . . . . . . . . . . . . . . . . . . . . . . . . . . . . . . . . . . . . . . . . . . . . . .45
Insect Collecting . . . . . . . . . . . . . . . . . . . . . . . . . . . . . . . . . . . . . . . . . . . . .46
Insect Killing and Relaxing Jars . . . . . . . . . . . . . . . . . . . . . . . . . . . . . . . .47
Insect Mounts . . . . . . . . . . . . . . . . . . . . . . . . . . . . . . . . . . . . . . . . . . . . . . .48
Insect Spreading Board . . . . . . . . . . . . . . . . . . . . . . . . . . . . . . . . . . . . . . .48
Jet Plane . . . . . . . . . . . . . . . . . . . . . . . . . . . . . . . . . . . . . . . . . . . . . . . . . . . .49
Lantern Slides . . . . . . . . . . . . . . . . . . . . . . . . . . . . . . . . . . . . . . . . . . . . . . .50
Leaf Collection . . . . . . . . . . . . . . . . . . . . . . . . . . . . . . . . . . . . . . . . . . . . . .51
Leaf Press . . . . . . . . . . . . . . . . . . . . . . . . . . . . . . . . . . . . . . . . . . . . . . . . . . .52
Lichens . . . . . . . . . . . . . . . . . . . . . . . . . . . . . . . . . . . . . . . . . . . . . . . . . . . . .53
Lift Pump . . . . . . . . . . . . . . . . . . . . . . . . . . . . . . . . . . . . . . . . . . . . . . . . . . .54
Light Bulb . . . . . . . . . . . . . . . . . . . . . . . . . . . . . . . . . . . . . . . . . . . . . . . . . . .54
Magnetic Crane . . . . . . . . . . . . . . . . . . . . . . . . . . . . . . . . . . . . . . . . . . . . .55
Marine Life . . . . . . . . . . . . . . . . . . . . . . . . . . . . . . . . . . . . . . . . . . . . . . . . . .56
Mice . . . . . . . . . . . . . . . . . . . . . . . . . . . . . . . . . . . . . . . . . . . . . . . . . . . . . . . .56
Microphotography . . . . . . . . . . . . . . . . . . . . . . . . . . . . . . . . . . . . . . . . . . .57
Microscopic Slides . . . . . . . . . . . . . . . . . . . . . . . . . . . . . . . . . . . . . . . . . . .58
Microtome . . . . . . . . . . . . . . . . . . . . . . . . . . . . . . . . . . . . . . . . . . . . . . . . . . .58
Mobiles . . . . . . . . . . . . . . . . . . . . . . . . . . . . . . . . . . . . . . . . . . . . . . . . . . . . .59
Moss Cycle . . . . . . . . . . . . . . . . . . . . . . . . . . . . . . . . . . . . . . . . . . . . . . . . . .60
Nature Center . . . . . . . . . . . . . . . . . . . . . . . . . . . . . . . . . . . . . . . . . . . . . . .61
Periscope . . . . . . . . . . . . . . . . . . . . . . . . . . . . . . . . . . . . . . . . . . . . . . . . . . . .62
Photometer . . . . . . . . . . . . . . . . . . . . . . . . . . . . . . . . . . . . . . . . . . . . . . . . . .62
Planetarium . . . . . . . . . . . . . . . . . . . . . . . . . . . . . . . . . . . . . . . . . . . . . . . . . .63
Prism . . . . . . . . . . . . . . . . . . . . . . . . . . . . . . . . . . . . . . . . . . . . . . . . . . . . . . .64
Radio . . . . . . . . . . . . . . . . . . . . . . . . . . . . . . . . . . . . . . . . . . . . . . . . . . . . . . .64
Reptiles . . . . . . . . . . . . . . . . . . . . . . . . . . . . . . . . . . . . . . . . . . . . . . . . . . . . .65
Respiratory Model . . . . . . . . . . . . . . . . . . . . . . . . . . . . . . . . . . . . . . . . . . .66
Rheostat . . . . . . . . . . . . . . . . . . . . . . . . . . . . . . . . . . . . . . . . . . . . . . . . . . . . .67
Rhythm Band . . . . . . . . . . . . . . . . . . . . . . . . . . . . . . . . . . . . . . . . . . . . . . . . .68
Salamanders . . . . . . . . . . . . . . . . . . . . . . . . . . . . . . . . . . . . . . . . . . . . . . . . .69
Sand Pictures . . . . . . . . . . . . . . . . . . . . . . . . . . . . . . . . . . . . . . . . . . . . . . . .70
Skeleton Mounts . . . . . . . . . . . . . . . . . . . . . . . . . . . . . . . . . . . . . . . . . . . . .71

Snowflake Casts . . . . . . . . . . . . . . . . . . . . . . . . . . . . . . . . . . . . . . . . . 71
Sound Pipes . . . . . . . . . . . . . . . . . . . . . . . . . . . . . . . . . . . . . . . . . . . . 72
Spider Webs . . . . . . . . . . . . . . . . . . . . . . . . . . . . . . . . . . . . . . . . . . . . . 72
Spring Scale . . . . . . . . . . . . . . . . . . . . . . . . . . . . . . . . . . . . . . . . . . . . 73
Static Electricity Detector . . . . . . . . . . . . . . . . . . . . . . . . . . . . . . . . 74
Steam Engine . . . . . . . . . . . . . . . . . . . . . . . . . . . . . . . . . . . . . . . . . . . 75
Stethoscope . . . . . . . . . . . . . . . . . . . . . . . . . . . . . . . . . . . . . . . . . . . . . 75
Storage Battery . . . . . . . . . . . . . . . . . . . . . . . . . . . . . . . . . . . . . . . . . 76
Streetlights . . . . . . . . . . . . . . . . . . . . . . . . . . . . . . . . . . . . . . . . . . . . . 77
Telegraph Set . . . . . . . . . . . . . . . . . . . . . . . . . . . . . . . . . . . . . . . . . . 78
Telephone . . . . . . . . . . . . . . . . . . . . . . . . . . . . . . . . . . . . . . . . . . . . . . 79
Telescope . . . . . . . . . . . . . . . . . . . . . . . . . . . . . . . . . . . . . . . . . . . . . . 80
Terrariums . . . . . . . . . . . . . . . . . . . . . . . . . . . . . . . . . . . . . . . . . . . . . 80
Tree Growth . . . . . . . . . . . . . . . . . . . . . . . . . . . . . . . . . . . . . . . . . . . . 82
Turbine . . . . . . . . . . . . . . . . . . . . . . . . . . . . . . . . . . . . . . . . . . . . . . . . 83
Vegetable Garden . . . . . . . . . . . . . . . . . . . . . . . . . . . . . . . . . . . . . . . 84
Water Purification . . . . . . . . . . . . . . . . . . . . . . . . . . . . . . . . . . . . . . 85
Wind Tunnel . . . . . . . . . . . . . . . . . . . . . . . . . . . . . . . . . . . . . . . . . . . 86
Windlass . . . . . . . . . . . . . . . . . . . . . . . . . . . . . . . . . . . . . . . . . . . . . . . 86
Wood Specimens . . . . . . . . . . . . . . . . . . . . . . . . . . . . . . . . . . . . . . . . 87
Wormery . . . . . . . . . . . . . . . . . . . . . . . . . . . . . . . . . . . . . . . . . . . . . . . 87
Worms . . . . . . . . . . . . . . . . . . . . . . . . . . . . . . . . . . . . . . . . . . . . . . . . . 88
Xylophone . . . . . . . . . . . . . . . . . . . . . . . . . . . . . . . . . . . . . . . . . . . . . 89

Index . . . . . . . . . . . . . . . . . . . . . . . . . . . . . . . . . . . . . . . . . . . . . . . . . . 91

# ANIMAL HOUSES

Wild animals should be left in the wild. A selected few can be brought into the home or classroom for short-term study of animal behavior. Construct a cage or container large enough for the animal to exercise. Be sure proper food is available.

An insect cage can be constructed from hardware cloth, copper screening, or fiberglass rolled into a cylinder the desired height and diameter. Pour a layer of plaster of paris in a tinfoil pie plate that is slightly larger than the cylinder. Set one end of the cylinder into the plaster and let it harden. A second pie plate serves as the lid and can be held firmly in place by wiring it to the screening. A small potted plant inside provides the insects with a place to climb, hide, or eat.

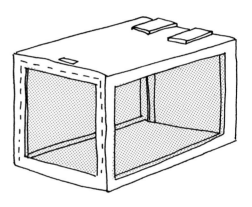

A snake house should be made of glass or smooth wood. A snake can damage its skin by rubbing against wire or sharp wooden edges in a cage. An old aquarium works well. A one- or two-gallon glass jug turned on its side in a wooden cradle will serve as a home for small reptiles. Make certain you provide floor coverings similar to their natural habitats—grassy sod and water for frogs, a bed of sand for lizards.

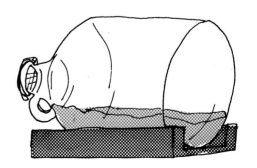

Larger animals, such as rabbits, guinea pigs, or white rats, need sturdy cages. They can be constructed from scrap lumber and 17-gauge hardware cloth of a least one-half-inch mesh. Follow the diagrams for sizes and patterns.

## ANIMAL TRACKS

Fill a backpack with a small sack of plaster of paris, a jar of water, spoon, small brush, and cardboard cylinders. Take a hike to the woods, along a stream bank or pond after rain when animals leave prints in the mud. When a footprint of some animal is discovered on the ground, carefully brush the print clean of any loose particles or debris. Place a cylinder of cardboard around it and push slightly into the soil. Mix some water with the plaster to the consistency of pudding. Pour this mixture over the track to a depth of one inch and let the material harden.

Remove the mold and clean off the soil. Back at home or school, grease the negative (raised) print with petroleum jelly. Place another cylinder of cardboard

around the mold so that it extends an inch above the level of the negative print. Pour a mixture of plaster on top of the first mold. When this hardens, separate the two pieces. The second casting is a positive print (depression) of the animal's footprint.

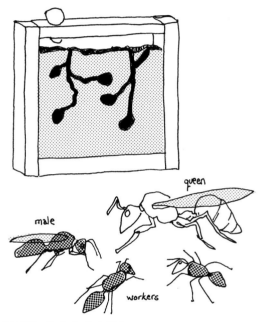

queen

male

workers

## ANT COLONY

An ant home can be made from two sheets of clear plastic. Tape one-inch-square pieces of wood on the sides, top, and bottom to keep the plastic separated. Drill a hole in the top piece of wood through which food and water can be added. A cotton plug in the hole will keep the ants inside. Keep the top piece movable for stocking the colony. Tape the other edges.

Locate an anthill. Dig up one square foot of soil around it. Place the soil and ants on a piece of white cloth. Examine the contents until the queen is located. The workers will not live without the queen in the colony. Transfer the colony to the new home. A newspaper funnel can be used to get ants and soil from the cloth into the narrow structure. Cover the glass with dark paper for two weeks to encourage the ants to make tunnels and rooms near the sides. This will make it easy to observe them. Place honey, sugar water, and a wet sponge on top of the soil line. The ants can live off this food.

## AQUARIUM PROJECTION

The excitement of watching a hydra extend its tentacles to grab a swimming daphnia (water flea) is worth the time needed to set up this tiny water cell.

Locate two 2″ x 2″ glass slides that fit into a slide projector, an attachment that comes with most classroom filmstrip projectors. Cut two wooden kitchen matches two inches long. Glue them together on opposite sides of one glass slide. Cut a third match slightly shorter to glue across the bottom. Put a little glue along the top of all exposed wood and place a second slide on top. Tape all three sides with a narrow strip of waterproof aquarium tape. You should end up with a thin glass aquarium the width of a wooden match and with the top side open.

Stock the aquarium with a variety of tiny plants and animals, such as hydra, water fleas, snails, baby guppies, algae, planaria, etc. Any plant or animal that lives in water and is small enough to fit between the glass slides can be included.

The aquarium is ready to be magnified. Carefully set it in the slide carrier of the projector and shoot the light onto a large screen . The heat and light from the projector bulb causes the tiny creatures to move rapidly. The little hydra looks like a large stinging monster when enlarged. The outer covering of the daphnia (water flea) is so transparent one can see the algae going down its digestive tract. If it gets too near the hydra, the food chain continues. The hydra eats the daphnia.

---

### DEFINITIONS

**daphnia** — a water flea that is only a few millimeters in size, lives in fresh waters, and is usually reddish in color; a crustacean

**hydra** — a freshwater animal that rarely exceeds a half-inch long, with stinging cells on its tentacles; in phylum Coelenterata

**planaria** — a flatworm that grows up to three inches long, usually gray or black; in phylum Platyhelminthes

---

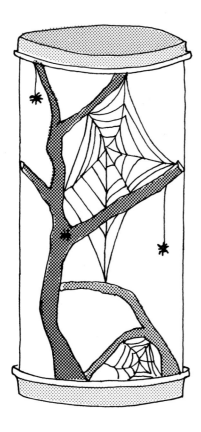

their new home. In the fall the egg cases of spiders also may be collected.

Arachnids need water daily but can go for weeks without food. Keep a wet sponge in the cage and occasionally drop in live, soft-bodied insects, such as flies or mealworms.

Spiders will live and reproduce in captivity. There are only a few poisonous spiders around, such as the black widow, brown recluse, and tarantula. Learn to recognize and stay away from poisonous spiders. Only the harmless ones should be selected as pets.

---

**DEFINITIONS**

**arachnid** — a class of animals in the phylum Arthropoda. Most live on land and have four pairs of walking legs.

---

## ARACHNIDS

Arachnids are fascinating animals to observe. They include spiders, scorpions, daddy longlegs, ticks, and mites.

Construct a cage by putting a cylinder of fine wire mesh upright in a cake pan of wet plaster of paris. Allow it to harden. Use another round cake pan as a removable cover. Insert several sticks to which spiders can attach their webs.

In the grass of open fields and under logs or rocks, many species of arachnids can be found. You might even find one crawling the walls of your bedroom. Capture them in a jar to transport to

## BALANCE SCALE

A balance scale is an instrument designed to compare an unknown weight with a known one. If one object is heavier, the beam will not balance.

Pattern your construction from the illustration. Use flat-headed screws to fasten the uprights to the base. They must be flush with the bottom so the balance will not tilt. The nut and bolt going through the top ends of the uprights should fit snugly. The hole in the balancing beam, however, should be slightly larger than the circumference of the bolt to permit the beam to move without friction. This hole must be in the exact center of the balance beam for the scale to weigh accurately. Hammer a nail in each end of the beam. Suspend foil pie tins from the nails by strings. Make certain the pans are the same size and the strings the same length. Little plastic toy pails would also work. Before you use this instrument be sure you have a perfect "balance."

A variety of objects at the hardware store can be used as weights, such as nuts, plumb bobs, curtain weights, and similar metal pieces. Weigh each one, and paint the ounces or pounds on it.

There are many times when experiments call for different quantities of various chemicals. These can be weighed rather accurately on your homemade scales.

Compare the weights of equal measurements of sugar, water, iron filings, flour, and cotton. Draw conclusions from your recordings.

---

### DEFINITIONS

**circumference** — the distance around the outer edge or perimeter of a circle

---

## BALL BEARINGS

---

Locate two metal cans that have deep grooves around their tops. Set one can on a table. Invert the other can and set it on top of the first can. Give it a turn. Notice the amount of friction between the two cans. Line the groove around the top of the first can with marbles and replace the second can on top so that the marbles fit partly in its grooves also. Turn the second can. Notice how much more easily it turns. You have used marbles in the same way ball bearings are used to reduce friction where one surface rubs against another. What effect does oiling the marbles have on the way the can turns?

When you first learned to roller skate you probably had beginner's skates. They have only one bearing and produce a lot of friction, but they prevent you from taking a lot of spills. Ball bearings on advanced skates have a circle of balls around the axle on each wheel. Examine both types of skates. Often if one shakes a pair of speed skates the rattle of the ball bearings can be heard.

## BELT-DRIVEN MACHINES

Collect four different sized, empty spools that once held sewing thread. Record the radius of each spool or wheel. Push a thumbtack into the top of each spool near the edge. The tack can be used to note one rotation. Cut an eight-inch square board to serve as a base. Hammer a long nail into each corner of the base. Set a spool on each nail. Loop a rubber band around two of the spools. Turn the larger spool one full turn. How much did the small wheel rotate? In what direction did it turn in relation to the large wheel? Can you figure out how to make the small wheel go in the opposite direction?

Experiment with all four wheel sizes. Use several rubber bands. Calculate the rotations as to size. Can you figure out a ratio that would work if you had larger or smaller spools? Look under a hood of an automobile. Ask a garage mechanic to explain what all the belts do.

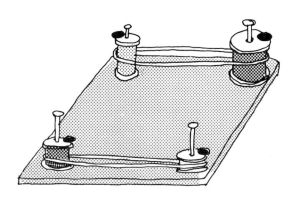

## BIRDHOUSES

Old unpainted wood is the best material for bird homes. Metal and wire get too hot in the summer and freeze a bird's feet in the winter. If you prefer paint be sure to use green, brown, or gray because birds are attracted by nature's colors. Set the house out in the fall so it will weather before spring occupancy. Pine, poplar, or cypress are woods that can be worked easily. Lumber mills can provide scraps with bark still on. This adds a rustic touch to a house and gives the young a rough surface to climb up to the entrance hole.

Roofs should be sloped to permit runoff of rain and covered with roofing paper or shingles. A couple of holes bored through the floor will prevent any standing water that seeps inside. Drill a few holes near the top of the walls just under the roof. This provides cross-ventilation. A small box with only one entrance hole can get pretty hot in the summer months when the mother bird is nesting.

The size of the house varies somewhat for different species of birds. On the average the inside of the house should measure at least 6″ x 6″ and be 8″ to 10″ high. The entrance or hole should be nearer the top and measure 1½″ to 2″ in diameter. The house should be anchored to a tree or post from six to ten feet above ground level.

Early in the spring give the nesting parents a helping hand. Place materials such as yarn, rags, string, twigs, wood shavings, and scraps of paper on the ground near the house. This will encourage and speed up nest building.

The adjoining diagrams provide a few patterns. A robin likes a three-sided house, a wren a single story; a purple martin lives in an apartment building, while a woodpecker chooses a ranch style dwelling.

---

**DEFINITIONS**

**diameter** — the distance through the center of an object or opening

---

water. Pour equal parts of these solutions into a pan. Let a sheet of paper float in the solution for several seconds. Hang the paper in a dark room to dry. It is now sensitized for blueprinting.

Place an object on the paper and expose it to sunlight for a few moments, depending upon the directness of the sun's rays. In summer it works in about thirty seconds. Exposure to winter sunlight may take five minutes. As soon as the blue around the object on the paper fades, the reaction is sufficient. Quickly immerse the paper in a pan of water. This "sets" the picture. Place the blueprint between sheets of paper towels until it is dry.

## BONE AND MUSCLE MODEL

This is a working model used to demonstrate how muscles move and control bones.

Drill a hole in one corner of one piece of plywood. Round the ends of the other piece and drill a hole in each end. Put in the screw eyes and cup hooks as shown in the illustration. Fasten the two pieces of wood together with a nut and bolt.

Locate a long and strong rubber band or something similar. Thread it through the screw eyes and around the cup hooks. The last step is to thread a cord from the cup hook on the top of the model through the screw eyes. Pull on the cord and the model will work in much the same way as the muscles and bones of your arm work when you bend your elbow. The

## BLUEPRINTING

Blueprint paper has been treated with chemicals so that it is sensitive or reacts when exposed to sunlight. It can be purchased at science supply houses or photographic shops. If you want to be a real scientist you should make your own. Here is the recipe.

Prepare two solutions in an almost dark room. First, mix ten grams of potassium ferricyanide (from a drugstore) with fifty milliliters of water. Then mix nineteen grams of ferric ammonium citrate (from a drugstore) with fifty milliliters of

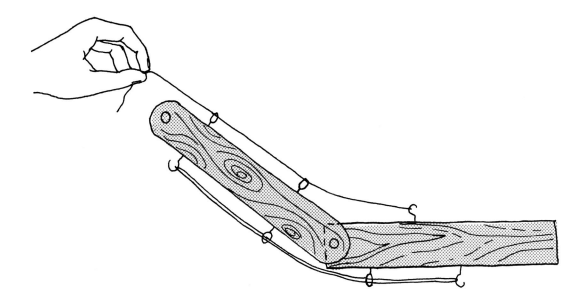

cord plays the role of the biceps muscle and the rubber band the triceps muscle.

To show the true length and attachment of the triceps you would need to add the shoulder. It is attached to the scapula and ulna bones. When the triceps contracts it lowers or depresses the upper arm and extends the elbow. It is a great muscle to help you do the backstroke while swimming. Can you figure out where other muscles are attached and how they help you perform certain activities? Some muscles will flex, others will extend, adduct, abduct, elevate, or rotate.

## DEFINITIONS

**abduct** — to move an appendage, such as an arm or leg, away from the center of the body

**adduct** — to move an appendage toward the center of the body

**scapula** — the shoulder blade, a triangular bone on the dorsal side of higher animals, a part of the pectoral girdle

**ulna** — a long, slender bone in the forearm on the little finger side, one end of which is the elbow; longer than the radius bone

## BURNER USING ALCOHOL

Many scientific experiments require a source of heat. Hot plates and propane jets are expensive. A homemade burner can serve the purpose.

Use a small jam or olive jar with a screw-on lid. A slit in the lid will hold the wick. Place the lid top side down on the ground or on a piece of softwood. Using a hammer and screwdriver make a slit in the center of the lid. Purchase a piece of lamp wick at a hardware store. Feed the wick through the slit so it extends one-half inch above the lid. Pour Ditto fluid or wood alcohol into the jar. Screw on the lid with the wick submerged in the fluid. The burner is ready to be used for experiments. Since the chemicals evaporate rapidly, wrap foil over the soaked wick and lid when you aren't using the heating device.

## CAMERA

A homemade camera may not win a prize in photography but it will provide an understanding of how a camera works.

Drill a half-inch hole in one end of a cigar box. Find a cork that fits tightly into this hole. On the inside of the box tape a one-inch by one-inch piece of foil over the hole. Take a needle and punch a clean pinhole directly in the center of the foil.

In a darkroom tape a piece of black-and-white photographic film on the end of the box directly opposite the needle hole. Fasten the lid of the box tightly with tape, and be certain the cork is in place before going out in the daylight.

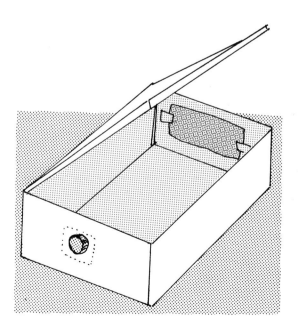

Point the camera at an object. Rest it on something to keep it from jiggling and distorting the picture. Remove the cork for one or two seconds depending on the brightness of the day and the speed of the film. Quickly replace the cork, return to the darkroom, and develop the film.

Chemicals, paper, containers, and instructions for developing film can be purchased at local photographic shops. Beginners should learn to develop black-and-white film before they tackle the more complicated task of working with color prints.

## CATERPILLARS

You will need an identification book to distinguish the larvae and pupae of butterflies and moths. Often the color of a larva is similar to the adult it will become.

Collect caterpillars (larvae), the chrysalises (pupae) of several species of butterflies, or the cocoons of moths. (Note the leaves of the plants where they are found—this is their food.) Place them in a container and leave it outside through the winter months. If they are brought inside in the fall adult butterflies or moths will emerge around December

when no food is available. They may be refrigerated until late winter. In a warm place they will come out of the pupae in two months or so. If your specimens are left outside during the winter, then in the early spring transfer them to an insect cage. Sprinkle them weekly. When adults emerge, supply them with fresh leaves. Each species prefers certain plants. Set them free when the study and observation of their life cycle have been completed.

---

### DEFINITIONS

**larva** — (plural, larvae) the second stage in the change of insects as they mature into adults. Caterpillars, maggots, and mealworms are larvae of certain insects.

**pupa** — (plural, pupae) the third stage in the change of some insects as they mature into adults, often the quiet or resting stage

# CELL MODELS

Embryology is the study of the development of an animal from a single fertilized egg to the stage of hatching or birth.

Use the adjoining diagrams to make a few of the representative stages of frog development. Mold each stage out of modeling clay. Stages E, F, H, and K each should be formed as a half ball to show the cross section of cellular growth and the structures forming on the inside. Use a knife or pencil to carve the outlines of the cells, cavities, germ layers, and systems that are evident at each stage.

A stand can be constructed for each model by inserting the clay form on the top end of a six-inch piece of dowel rod. Bases can be made from cross sections of a dead tree branch. Drill a hole in the top of each to insert the dowel rod. Titles for each stage can be taped on the top of the base. Number each part to be identified on the model and then put the number key on the base also.

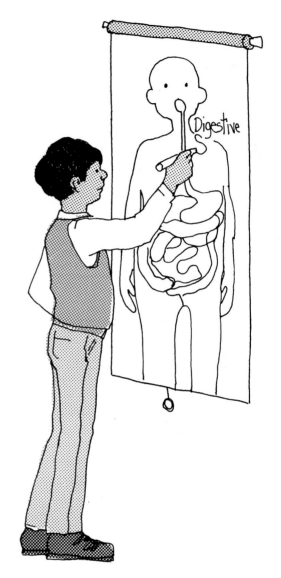

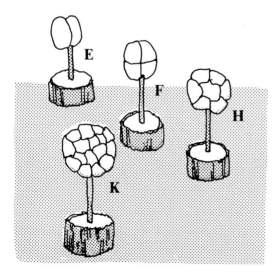

## CHARTS

Commercial classroom charts are expensive and often too complex for a young scientist to understand. Making your own lets you simplify their structure and concepts. It also gives you a chance to combine artistic talent with scientific background.

Window shades are excellent for this project. Paper shades are cheaper but linen ones are more durable. Decide on the length and mount the brackets on a board in the classroom. The surface of the shade will take drawings of crayon, felt pen, water colors, oil paints, or ink. Make a pencil sketch of all diagrams, pictures, and text on the chart before you use permanent markers. Later the pencil marks can be erased. If you're not too adept at drawing, pictures projected on the window shade will let you trace artwork.

Here are a few ideas for charts: the systems of the human body, one-celled animals found in a drop of pond water, the geologic timetable, plant and animal kingdoms, layers of the atmosphere and cloud heights, space explorations, simple machines, and electrical pathways of series and parallel circuits.

## CHICKEN BROODER

A brooder can be made from an old orange crate that is divided into two "rooms." Cover the sides and top with chicken wire. Remember to make an opening on top through which you can feed and water the chicks daily. Box in one room with cardboard. Put a hanging light in it with a 25-watt bulb for heat when the temperature goes down at night. Cut a little doorway in the middle partition so the chickens can go from one room to the other. In the exposed room or yard, place an upside-down feeder, mash, and scratch. The mash and scratch can be purchased at a local feed store. A little straw or dried grass scattered on the floor in both rooms will add to the comfort of the young birds.

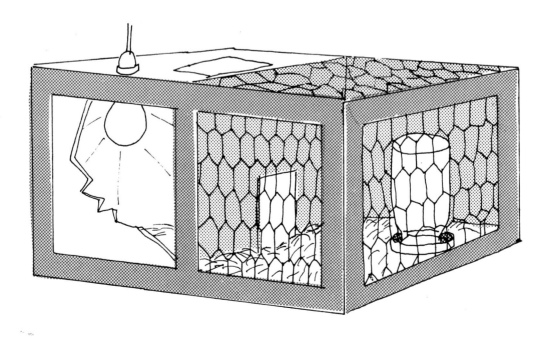

## CHROMATOGRAPHY

The separating of a mixture into its various parts by letting it be absorbed by a solid, such as filter paper, is called chromatography. Different molecules in a mixture travel at different speeds depending upon absorption and ion exchange. Scientists use this technique to identify unknown compounds. The relative distances and flow rate can be calculated. The following setup introduces the techniques used by a chromatographer.

Use a jam jar or similar jar with a lid. Cut a strip of filter paper slightly longer than the length of the jar. Tape one end to the center of the inside of the cap. The opposite end should touch the bottom of the jar. Place a drop of blue-black ink in the middle of the filter paper, one-half way up the strip. After the ink dries, pour a little water in the bottom of the jar. Screw on the cap. The bottom end of the paper should be in the water. Observe the rate of absorption. What happens to the ink spot when the water reaches it? Repeat the test using alcohol instead of water. Next try food coloring in place of the ink.

For a more interesting mixture for color separation, use plant pigments. Test a variety of different leaves: geranium, coleus, spinach, beet, etc. Petals of flowers may also be used. The pigment solution is made by placing several leaves of a plant in a test tube half full of water and boiling for a minute or two. Pour this into a small dish with a little sand and acetone. Use a wooden spoon to grind this mixture so the pigments can be separated from the plant cells. (A mortar and pestle will do the best grinding job.) Pour the mixture through filter paper. Using the setup prepared previously pour the filtrate into the bottom of the jar. Screw on the lid with the hanging strip of filter paper and watch the pigments being absorbed at different rates and the colors separate at different heights on the paper. What is the order of these pigments on your chromatogram: carotene (yellow-orange), chlorophyll (green), and xanthophyll (yellow-red)?

---

### DEFINITIONS

**ion exchange** — an atom or group of atoms that have lost or gained electrons; may have a positive or negative charge

# CIRCULATION

Collect half a dozen friends to help play this game that follows a drop of blood through the body.

Make seven signs out of 6″ x 8″ cards, punching two holes on the top to insert a string. Hang the signs from the players' necks. Print one of the following on each sign in the color designated: right atrium (blue), right ventricle (blue), left atrium (red), left ventricle (red), right lung and left lung (any color but red or blue), and finally blood (red) on one side of a card and blood (printed in blue) on the opposite side.

Position the players with the two ventricles in front of the two atria and far enough away from each other so that the four chambers of the heart do not touch when the players' arms are extended out to the sides. Get the heart started to a rhythm of LUB-dup. The ventricle players will contract by wrapping their arms around their own chests. At the same time the atrium players extend their arms to the sides. This is the relaxed position when the blood can enter. Now alternate so that the ventricles relax and the atria contract. Position the two lung players on either side of the heart. The blood player should be at the other end of the room, starting from the "big toe." The blood sign printed in blue should be showing.

As the heart is beating smoothly and slowly, the blood player will walk to the heart, step into the right atrium when the arms are extended, but step back out as the atrium contracts. Where does the blood go next? When the blood player leaves the lung, his sign should be flipped over to the red side since it has been oxygenated. The blood player must get in and out of all four chambers and lung before he can go back to the "big toe." If your friends get mixed up playing this game, call for a heart transplant and get other players!

23

## COMPASS TRAVELS

A compass is an instrument with a swinging magnetic needle. Since the same end of the needle always points north, it is used to show direction. A compass is an important tool in mapmaking. It has 360 degrees marked on the circle around the magnet. Each degree is a direction and often is referred to as an azimuth.

The Silva-System compass is an excellent one for beginners. The fluid-filled compass housing is fastened to a rectangular plastic base. The base has a travel arrow outside the compass and an orienting arrow underneath the housing. Inches and millimeters are marked along two edges.

Let's learn to walk a straight path to the north. Hold the compass in your hands, waist high, with your forearms resting on your hips. This will keep the compass level and always in the same position in relation to your body. Turn the orienting arrow until it points to N on the compass. Turn around until the red end of the magnet also points north, floating above the orienting arrow. Hold the housing with one hand while you rotate the base to line up the travel arrow with the orienting arrow and the north-seeking magnetic arrow. This is your direction of travel. To insure a true walk to the north look up from the travel arrow and spot an object in the distance that you will head for, such as a tree, light pole, or rock. When you arrive at this object, recheck your compass. It still should be pointing to the north.

Try traveling in several directions using the compass. Line up all arrows to the north. Drive a stake in the ground at this starting point. Turn the base until the travel arrow is on 90 degrees. Face in this direction. Be sure the red end of the magnet is floating over the orienting arrow in the housing. Walk twenty steps at this azimuth. Drive a second stake here. Turn the base to 180 degrees and orient your compass to north. Walk twenty steps and stake it. Turn the base to 270 degrees and repeat. Finally set your direction at 360 degrees; you should be heading back to your starting spot. Look at your stakes. If you used the compass correctly you have walked a square.

Using these techniques see if you can figure out the shape of the following two sets of directions.

Set your arrows on north. Taking twenty steps on each leg of your journey, travel 30 degrees, then 150 degrees, and finally 270 degrees. Remember to orient your compass to the north at each turn and drive a stake in the ground when you change direction. What geometrical shape did you walk?

Here is a longer and more difficult math hike. Orient the compass to the north. Taking twenty steps in each direction travel 360 degrees, 300 degrees, 240 degrees, 180 degrees, 120 degrees, and finally 60 degrees. You made a shape with how many angles? What is the name of this geometric pattern?

Use your compass to set up a treasure hunt for a group of friends.

## COMPOST PILE

Organic gardeners prefer compost fertilizer to commercial chemicals. It is necessary to start the pile the year before you will want to use it.

Choose a hidden, shady corner of the yard. Dig a shallow pit and erect a wire fence around the hole. It should be low enough for you to reach over it to turn the rotting material every month or so.

Fill the hole with grass cuttings, a little kitchen garbage of vegetable and fruit peels, sifted wood ashes from a fireplace, dead leaves, cornstalks, or any other organic material available. Wet it down with a sprinkler. When the contents of the pile have disintegrated into fine pieces (after several months), the compost is ready to be worked into the soil. You are returning to the soil the elements necessary for the growth of plants. The compost will supply lime, phosphorus, potassium, nitrogen, and calcium.

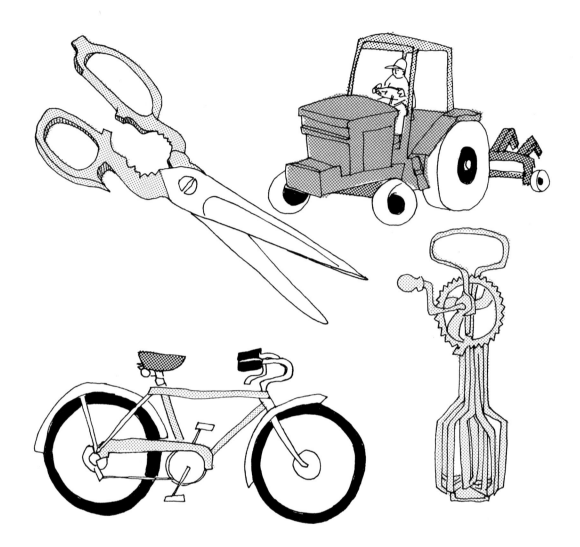

## COMPOUND MACHINES

After you are familiar with the six simple machines (wheel and axle, lever, inclined plane, screw, wedge, and pulley) and how they operate, you are ready to examine complex machines and tools. A complex one is composed of two or more simple ones.

Study a bicycle, motorcycle, automobile, hand eggbeater, meat grinder, gar-den clippers, lawn mower, tractor, hay lift, combine, table saw, etc. Take a pair of scissors as an example of a complex tool. A screw holds the halves together. You operate the handles as a lever to push two wedges through a material. Which is the most complex machine you found? Can you find a machine that has all six simple machines somewhere in its structure?

# DIAZO PAPER PRINTS

Diazo paper, also called Ozalid, is light sensitive. Unlike blueprinting paper it comes in a variety of colors. It can be purchased at any store that sells supplies for drafting. You will also need a bottle of household ammonia sold at grocery stores. The concentration of this chemical should be around 25 per cent. *Caution:* Do not breathe the fumes of ammonia, for it burns the respiratory tract.

Diazo paper usually comes in large sheets. In a dark room cut it into small pieces, such as 5-inch by 8-inch sheets, depending upon the size of the objects being printed. Set up a fixing jar before starting the printing process. Locate a wide-mouth jar slightly taller than the width of the diazo sheet. Put an inch of pebbles in the bottom. Pour in a half-inch layer of ammonia solution. Cap the jar until you are ready to use it.

Select specimens that have a distinctive shape in silhouette form. Leaves, winged seeds and pods, flowers, ferns, evergreen branches, and the magnetic field formed with a magnet and iron filings are all good choices. Keep the diazo paper wrapped in heavy paper when not in use. Take out a sheet, lay the specimen on it. Expose it to the sun for a minute or less depending on the time of the year and the color of the paper. Red diazo works faster than blue or black paper. The color around the object fades when the sun's rays strike it. Immediately remove the specimen and roll the paper up with the printed surface on the inside.

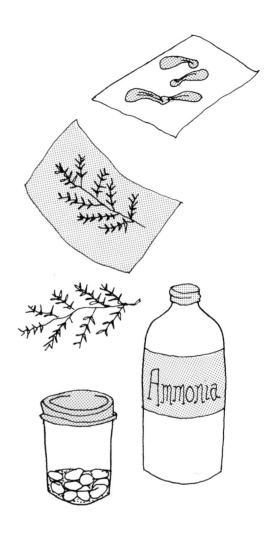

Set the roll in the fixing jar on top of the pebbles and reseal. The ammonia will set the color as it develops the picture. This process takes around five minutes. Overexposure to the fumes causes too dark a print while pale pictures need more time in the jar. Practice makes perfect.

## ECLIPSE VIEWER

During an eclipse of the moon an observer may look directly at the moon since it is reflecting sunlight. A lunar eclipse occurs when the earth moves between the sun and moon. A solar eclipse occurs when the moon in its revolution around the earth blocks the sun's rays to the earth. Never look directly at the sun. The invisible infrared rays can burn the retina in the back of the eye, causing partial or total loss of sight.

There are two ways to observe a solar eclipse indirectly. The pinhole camera described on page 18 can be used. No film is necessary. Cut a window on one side near the back or pinhole end to look inside the box. Point the pinhole in the direction of the sun. The eclipse can be viewed on the opposite end of the box through the window. The longer the box the better the image you will get.

An even simpler viewer requires only two pieces of cardboard. Make a pinhole in the one you will hold closest to you. With your back to the sun direct the sun's rays through the hole and onto the second cardboard, which should be held at arm's length. The eclipse is upside down. This is not apparent during a total eclipse but would be during a partial one. Remember, never look directly at a solar eclipse.

---

**DEFINITIONS**

**retina** — the inside back layer of the eyeball, containing the nerve endings that pick up images of black and white or color

---

## ELECTRIC QUIZ GAME

A young electrician can assemble this game to test the skills and knowledge of a group of friends on a rainy day when you are stuck inside.

First, decide on the subject of the game. It could be the identification of animals, plants, machines, rocks, etc. Collect pictures of these objects that can be glued to 2" x 3" pieces of cardboard. On 1" x 2" cardboards write the name of each object; for example, pictures of birds on the larger cards and the names of these birds on the smaller cards.

At a lumberyard purchase a sheet of pegboard large enough to hold at least

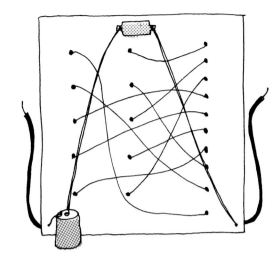

ten cards and ten answers with space in between. You will need a nut and bolt for each picture and answer. At a hardware store buy a roll of bell wire, a 1½ volt dry cell, a tiny bulb, and a light socket to hold it.

Follow the illustration to set up the front of the board. Punch holes in each card. Fasten them with a bolt through a hole in the pegboard. Arrange the pictures on the right and the answers down the left side. Fasten the little light socket and bulb at the top of the board with wire.

Now follow the diagram to wire the back of the game. Be sure to strip off the insulation on the ends of all contact points. Cut ten pieces of bell wire all the same length, the distance from one corner to the farthest corner. This will allow you to rearrange the pattern when you change the game plan. Wrap the end of a piece of bell wire around the bolt and secure it in place with the nut. Each wire should connect the picture of a bird to its name.

Cut three longer pieces of bell wire. Connect one to one side of the light socket, then through another hole to the front side. Connect the second wire from the other screw on the light socket to the center terminal of the dry cell. Connect the third wire to the outside terminal of the dry cell and run it through a hole in the pegboard to the front side. If done correctly you will have two free ends in front of your game board to play the quiz. Take the left wire and touch the bolt holding the robin picture. Then the right wire touching the word *robin* should make the bulb light up. The circuit is closed only when you touch the correct answer.

This game board can be used for subjects other than science, such as math problems, phonics skills, or geography. How many cards would you need for all the states and their capitals?

## ELECTRICAL SWITCH

Cut a metal strip one inch by four inches from a coffee can. Tape the sharp sides of the strip to avoid cutting yourself. Locate a block of wood about three inches by five inches. Hammer a nail into one end of the metal strip to make a hole in it. Bend three fourths of the strip at a right angle upward. Then bend two thirds of that piece down until it is parallel to the surface of the board. Screw it into the wooden base, leaving one-eighth inch of the screw sticking up. Put a screw in the other end of the wood beneath the end of the switch. Have it protrude enough so that it is one-quarter inch below the switch.

Wire your homemade knife switch in a parallel circuit with a light receptacle and a dry cell. Use a pencil or other non-conductor to push the metal strip down on the screw. If your construction is accurate you will see the light.

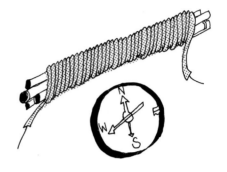

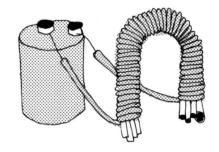

## ELECTROMAGNET

Cut several lengths of wire from clothes hangers. Wrap forty turns of bell wire around a bundle of the wire pieces, making sure you wrap in one direction. Remove the insulation from the two ends of the bell wire in order to make direct contact with the two terminals of a dry cell. Bend the bundle into a horseshoe shape. Experiment with the magnet when the electric circuit is complete. What materials will the electromagnet pick up? Test the poles with a compass to determine the north- and south-seeking poles.

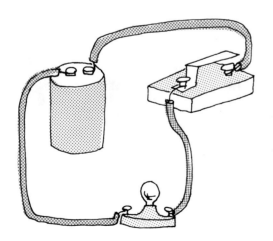

Can you make the horseshoe magnet do more work? First test the magnet with forty turns of wire. How many paper clips will it pick up? Wrap the bundles of wire pieces with eighty turns of bell wire. (You can continue with the first setup by taping the connection between the wires.) How many clips will this magnet attract? Repeat again using 120 turns. Is the outcome what you predicted?

## ELECTROSCOPE

An electroscope is a device that reacts if an object possesses an electrical charge. There are two ways to make an electroscope.

Crease a two-inch by eight-inch strip of newspaper and spread it on a table crease side up. Rub the surface hard with a piece of fur. This will give it a negative charge. Insert a pencil in the crease and hold up the paper strip. What happens to the ends of the paper? Now rub a rubber or plastic comb with the fur and hold it between the leaves of the paper. What kind of charge does the comb have?

A more complex electroscope requires a large glass jar and a cork soaked with wax that fits the jar exactly. Make a hook on the end of a copper wire large enough to hold a strip of aluminum foil.

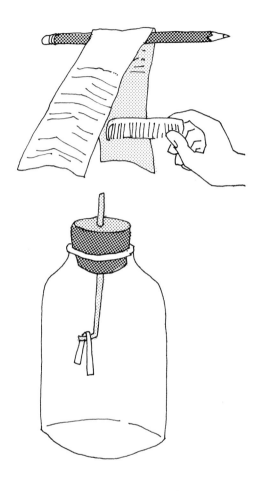

The foil from a stick of gum (if separated from the paper) works best because it is thin and light. Push the straight end of the wire through the cork so that it is outside the bottle. Rub a glass rod vigorously with a piece of nylon. Hold the rod close to the copper wire above the cork. What happens to the strip of foil inside the jar?

# ELEMENTS

Models of some of the common chemicals on the periodic table of elements can be assembled to provide a better understanding of their atomic structure.

Purchase a bag of miniature marshmallows of various colors. Dip white ones in food coloring to increase the number of colors. These will represent the electrons, protons, and neutrons in each element. The energy levels or orbits to hold the electrons around the nucleus can be fashioned out of circles of heavy string. Cut pieces of string that are ten, fifteen, twenty, etc., inches long. Soak each string in a bowl of glue. Form a circle of the string on wax paper or foil and let it dry.

Begin by assembling the first and simplest on the table, an atom of hydrogen. Cut a long piece of string to serve as a place to attach all the pieces of the atom

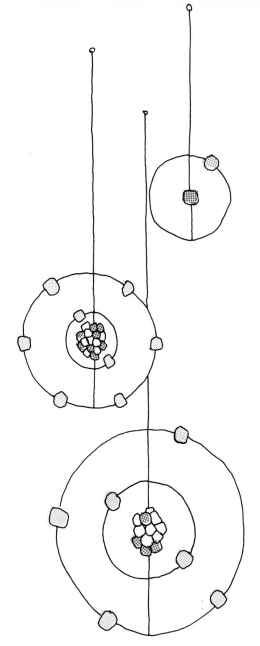

---

## DEFINITIONS

**electron** — a particle of an atom that carries a negative charge and orbits around the nucleus. A flow of electrons produces an electrical current.

**element** — a material that cannot be separated into different materials. It is made of atoms of the same kind and arranged on a periodic table in chemistry.

**neutron** — a particle of an atom that carries no charge, located in the nucleus

**nucleus** — the center or core of an atom, usually containing protons and neutrons, and around which the electrons revolve

**proton** — a particle of an atom that carries a positive charge, located in the nucleus

---

and to hang the finished product. Put a drop of glue on the ten-inch circle in one spot and a second spot directly opposite it. Stick this to the anchor string at the bottom as shown in the diagram. Glue a green marshmallow (proton) on the string in the center of the circle. Glue a pink marshmallow (electron) on a spot anywhere on the circle.

of the box tell you how many energy levels and the number of electrons in each level. For example, box number 11 is Na, or sodium. The vertical row of numbers is 2, 8, and 1. This requires three circles of string. The nucleus will be a cluster of eleven protons, eleven neutrons, plus eleven electrons orbiting around the nucleus at different levels. Any element more complex will need larger circles for the electron levels.

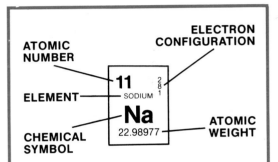

## HOW TO READ THE PERIODIC TABLE

All the elements are listed by their *atomic number*. The atomic number is the number of protons in the nucleus of an atom of the element.

The *chemical symbol* for the element can be the first two letters of the element's name, or the first two letters of its Latin or Greek name. (The Latin name for sodium is *natrium*.)

The *atomic weight* of an element is found by comparing its weight to the weight of carbon-12, an *isotope* of carbon.

A single atom of an element has different energy levels surrounding it. (You can imagine these levels as shells that fit one outside another.) In the first energy level of an atom the atom can have 2 electrons; in the second it can have 8; in the third, 18. Sodium has 2 electrons in its first energy level, 8 in its second, but only 1 in its third. When an energy level is not filled, the atom is very reactive, and tends to form compounds to share the electrons in energy levels that are not completely filled. The *electron configuration* tells how many electrons an atom of an element has.

Now assemble one that has two energy levels, such as oxygen, number eight on the periodic table. An atom of this element has eight protons, eight neutrons, and eight electrons. First glue a fifteen-inch circle to the anchor string. Glue a ten-inch circle inside it. Glue six pink electrons in the outer circle (energy level) and two pink electrons in the inner circle. Let this dry so it can be suspended with the anchor string. Then glue eight green protons and eight white neutrons in a cluster around the anchor string in the center of the inner energy level to form the nucleus. The oxygen atom is complete. If you make any element models with more than three energy levels, make circle strings at least five inches longer than the previous string.

Study a periodic chart and select elements to model. The smaller numbers listed in a vertical row on the right side

## EMBEDDING IN PLASTIC

Encasing delicate plants and animals in a bed of plastic preserves them for continued viewing and study. Embedding plastic may be obtained in a hobby-model shop or a science supply house. Directions for embedding are provided. It may be necessary to buy a hardening agent, thinning compound, and mold release, depending upon the complexity of the operation.

Select specimens that can be air dried before embedding, such as insects, flowers, grasses, shells, and starfish. Wet embedments require techniques using formalin and alcohol of different strengths—a process you can learn later.

Select a mold with sloped sides, such as a sauce dish or custard cup. Coat it with mold release. This is like greasing a pan so the cake pops out when turned over. Some plastic requires the addition of a catalyst to harden the plastic. Keep the lid on all containers except when pouring out the quantity needed.

Insects and other lightweight specimens have a tendency to float to the top of the liquid plastic. This requires layering—pouring in a small amount, placing the insect on top, and carefully holding it under the plastic for a few minutes with a dissecting pin or needle. It may be necessary to push the plastic around its legs and wings to prevent bubbles from clinging to the body. As soon as the plastic sets up like gel, another layer can be poured in.

Flowers, moths, and butterflies have a tendency to lose color. They can be laminated between plastic first or sprayed with several coats of clear plastic spray, which can be obtained in a paint or hardware store.

Work with a small mold and specimen until you learn the technique. Soon you will be able to embed a whole scene of life in a glass pie dish. The curing time depends upon the brand and depth of the cast. It may be completely hard in several days or can be dried in an oven at 45 degrees Celsius for five hours. The casting is finished off or polished with wet sandpaper.

# FERN CYCLE

A fern has to go through two generations to complete its life cycle. The asexual plant is the familiar one seen growing in the woods. The sexual plant is a tiny, heart-shaped plant seldom seen by nature lovers. You can grow both plants if you follow directions carefully.

The sporophyte generation (asexual) will thrive well in a bog terrarium. Have the new home established before you go fern hunting. Ferns are found in wooded areas along the banks of streams or in marshy environments. When you dig up a plant be sure the entire underground stem is taken with it. Wrap it in wet newspaper and transfer the plant to a bog terrarium. Keep the terrarium in a north window and water frequently.

To grow the second generation, the gametophyte (sexual), wait until spores appear on the underside of the fronds. Tap the compound leaf over a sheet of paper and the spores will fall off. Fill a pot with soil and peat moss. Put a layer of sand on top. Pour boiling water over the whole mixture and the container to destroy any bacteria or mold spores that will attack the germinating fern spores. Let it cool. Sprinkle the spores on the sand, cover the pot with clear plastic or glass, and set the pot in a saucer in order to water from the bottom up. In several weeks the spores will develop into tiny, heart-shaped gametophyte plants. These plants produce eggs and sperms. When a

sperm fertilizes an egg, a small fern sporophyte will grow out of this plant. When it is several inches tall, transfer it to the bog terrarium.

## DEFINITIONS

**asexual plant** — a plant containing cells that can reproduce without uniting with another cell; lacks sex cells

**egg** — the reproductive cell of most female animals and plants; unites with sperm or male cell to produce a new organism

**sexual generation** — one of two generations in the life cycle of some plants, in which eggs and sperms are produced and the fertilized egg grows into the asexual plant

**sperm** — the reproductive cell of most male animals and plants, that unites with an egg or female cell to produce a new organism

The female part, or pistil, will be in the center of the flower. With a sharp knife cut across the ovary at the base of the pistil. With a hand lens if the structure is tiny, count the number of chambers or carpels that contain the eggs. Draw a larger circle for the pistil with lines designating the number of carpels.

A perfect and complete flower has all four parts. If a flower lacks one or more it is incomplete. If it has only one sex it is imperfect. Be sure to examine a composite, such as a dandelion or carnation, that has many flowers on one flower stalk. A petunia, bluebell, and lily of the valley are examples of coalescence, the fusion of petals. A corn tassel is the male flower while the baby ear of corn is the female. What other interesting flowers can you find?

Collect a variety of specimens. Spring, summer, or fall will provide the collector with a variety of flowers, both cultivated and wild. Don't forget to take samples from shrubs and trees that are in bloom.

Begin by counting and drawing the outer ring of floral parts, the sepals. Use tweezers to pick them off. Count the next ring of parts, the petals. Use the shape of a quarter moon for diagraming the sepals and petals. Remove the petals to expose the stamens, or male structures. Use small circles to illustrate these.

## FLORAL DIAGRAMS

Studying and diagraming flower parts is important in the identification and classification of higher plants—the angiosperms. Botanists use a pattern that you can copy.

### DEFINITIONS

**angiosperms** — plants that produce flowers and fruits, further classified into monocots and dicots

# FLOWER PRESERVATION

Cut a leaf and flower from a plant. Care should be taken not to pull up or otherwise destroy valuable plants. Press the flower and leaf between paper that will absorb moisture. Newspaper is excellent. Change papers each day until the specimens are thoroughly dry. A plant press or weights placed on top will help smooth them out. Mount specimens in a scrapbook or on cardboard, using transparent tape. Label each specimen with the name of the plant, habitat, place collected, and date.

Clear plastic sheets are available that can be sealed with a hot iron. This is called lamination. Flowers enclosed in plastic are not destroyed by insects.

Flowers can also be dried in borax, a compound sold in grocery stores. The box you use must be taller than the upright flower. Stand the flower in the box using a flower holder to keep it centered and upright. Pour the borax gently around the flower until it is buried. Make sure the branches and petals maintain their natural positions. It will take a week for a delicate flower to dry and several weeks for a thick, succulent one. When the specimen is thoroughly dry pour off the borax carefully. Save it to use again. Dried flowers can be arranged into bouquets and enjoyed all winter.

Do not collect any specimen that is on the endangered species list. This list is available free from the Department of Conservation in most state capitals.

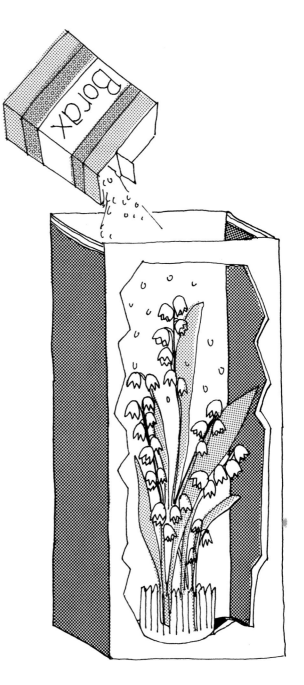

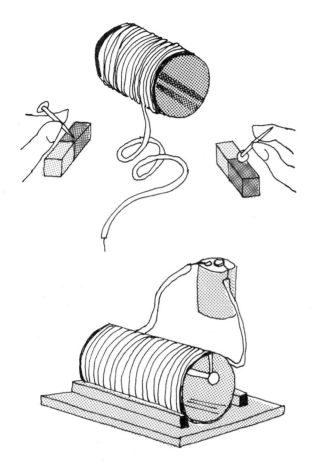

end of the magnet. Tie a string around the nail and tape the other end of the string to the top of the salt box. The apparatus you have just made is a galvanometer. Place it parallel to the earth's poles. Remove an inch of insulation from the two ends of wire and connect them from the coil to a dry cell. The nail will swing to a position parallel to the coil of wire.

To use the galvanometer above, substitute a commercial compass for the homemade one, the magnetized nail. Attach another coil of wire to the coil around the compass. The connecting wires should be at least five feet long so the magnet isn't close enough to the compass to affect it directly. Move a magnet rapidly in and out of the coil while you watch the current detector. Does the needle move? If it does, it indicates you are generating a current in the coil by moving the magnet in and out of it. Does the same thing happen when you hold the magnet still and move the coil on and off the pole of the magnet?

## GALVANOMETER

Cut an end out of an empty salt box and wrap about twenty-five feet of bell wire around the box. Leave one foot of the wire ends free. Nail two small pieces of wood to a block of wood. The coil of wire will lie on this base. Magnetize a thin finishing nail by stroking one end on the south end of a bar magnet. Stroke the other end of the nail on the north

## GRAFTING PLANTS

Grafting is a technique used by gardeners to attach the growing part of one plant to another living plant in order to develop new characteristics. It is not difficult to do if you follow certain basic rules.

Graft plants only in the winter or spring when the plants are dormant. The stock (base part) and the scion (part of

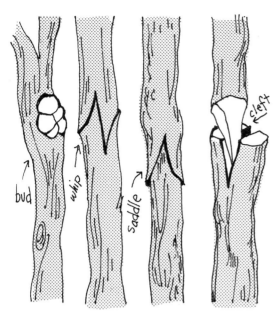

another plant to be grafted) should belong to the same species. For example, a branch of a Delicious apple tree can be grafted to a Winesap apple tree but not to a cherry tree. Be sure that the cambium (growing layer) of the scion and stock touch each other. Select only strong, healthy plants free from apparent disease. Cover the joined parts with a wax and wrap securely to prevent water loss and to keep the scion in place. A wax can be made with four parts resin, two parts beeswax, one part tallow, and one-half part linseed oil. Combine all ingredients and heat. Apply with a brush when slightly cool.

## GREENHOUSE

If you live in a cold climate, it is possible to grow indoor tropical plants, such as crotons, orchids, caladiums, sundews, Venus's-flytraps, and pitcher plants.

They need more moisture than ordinary room air provides. It is not difficult to build a greenhouse that has the proper atmosphere.

Plan to put it on the south side of a room where it will get morning sun. Use storm windows for the sides of the greenhouse. Stand three of them on end and nail together to form three sides. The fourth window is used as a door. Hinge it to one of the sides and secure it with a hook and eye. Half of a storm window will form the top of the structure if nailed to the three side walls. You can build shelves on one side for small potted plants. Tall plants can be placed on the floor. Keep the plants well watered and spray the inside of the greenhouse with water several times a week.

## GUINEA PIGS

Guinea pigs are quite clean and odor free and make good pets. They will thrive on a diet of guinea pig or rabbit pellets. Supplement this with nuts, grains, and vegetable greens.

A cage can be constructed with wire mesh and a wooden base. Use a large cookie sheet for the floor. It can be pulled out for easy cleaning. Guinea pigs enjoy rooting around in shredded newspaper, which also soaks up urine. A small wooden box inside the cage will serve as a hiding place for your pets. Use a shallow food dish and a wide-mouthed water jar. Wire the water jar into a corner of the cage. Give the animals fresh water daily. Keep the cage at room temperature and away from drafts and full sun. Guinea pigs mate and raise their

offspring in captivity. Gestation period is sixty-five to seventy days. A litter may include one to six babies.

---

**DEFINITIONS**

**gestation** — the period or length of time that a female animal carries the young in the uterus, often called pregnancy

---

## GUPPIES

Prepare an aquarium allowing at least a gallon of water for every pair of guppies. Supply ample plant life to provide adequate hiding places for the young. The mother guppy eats many things, including her offspring. Do not let the water temperature fall below 70 degrees

Fahrenheit or exceed 100 degrees. Guppies thrive in warm water.

Guppies are live-bearers. When a female guppy is about to produce young, or is gravid, place it in another aquarium immediately. It takes three to four weeks for a brood to appear after mating. Feed guppies commercial fish food, daphnia, or brine shrimp. Do not overfeed.

---

**DEFINITIONS**

**gravid** — pregnant; the stage when offspring are carried in the female body

---

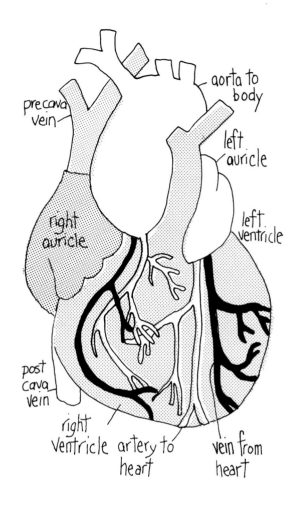

## HEART INSIDE AND OUT

---

Purchase an animal's heart (beef, sheep, or veal) at the grocery store. Select one that has the longest vessels still attached to it. Try to determine the right and left sides before you cut into it to expose the chambers and valves. Usually the large vessel curving over the top of the atria will be the aorta. Carefully push a pencil or small stick down into it until it ends in a chamber. This will be the left ventricle. The other large vessel on top branching into two arteries is the pulmonary artery leading into each lung. It leads out from the right ventricle.

Now with a sharp scissors cut through the muscle on the two sides and around the bottom. Leave uncut the top of the heart where all the vessels go in and out. Using your probe locate the vena cava entering the right atrium and the pulmonary arteries leading into the left atrium. Locate the tricuspid valve on the right and the mitral valve on the left side. Compare the thickness of the chamber walls. Why must the ventricle wall be the largest and strongest? How does the composition of the blood differ from the right side to the left side? Where has the blood come from and where is it going?

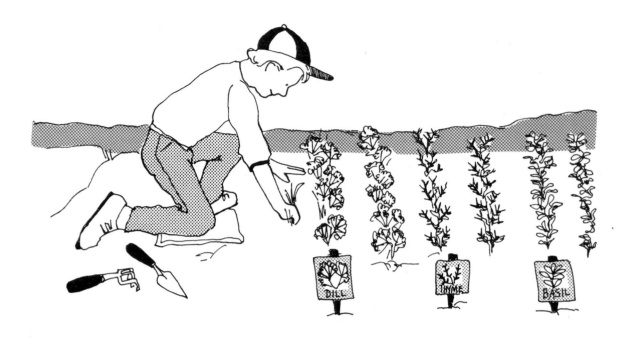

## HERB GARDEN

An herb is a nonwoody plant. More commonly we think of herbs as those plants from which we obtain spices, seasonings, or medicine. Herbage vegetables contain more minerals, proteins, and vitamins than they do carbohydrates.

Follow the directions for growing a vegetable garden in preparing the soil, fertilizing, planting, and maintenance. Stores that sell seeds usually have a good choice of herbs. They often carry seeds of basil, sage, thyme, tarragon, garlic, dill, pepper, mustard, and mint. Research which part of the plant is used for seasoning—the root, stem, leaf, flower, fruit, or seed.

## HEREDITY

Have you ever wondered why your eyes or hair are the color they are? Did you inherit the colors from your mother, father, or a grandparent? Physical traits are carried from one generation to another in little cell bodies called chromosomes. Smaller parts of chromosomes are the genes that are responsible for what you look like.

This project will take some time, for you may have to write many letters or call relatives. Ask them to look up or recall the physical appearance of people. First, decide which characteristics you want to chart. Some traits you might follow are color of hair and eyes, height, curly or straight hair, shape of the nose, baldness, color blindness, etc. Then find out what each of your relatives looked like and put all the data on a large chart. When you finish you may have a better understanding of why you look as you do.

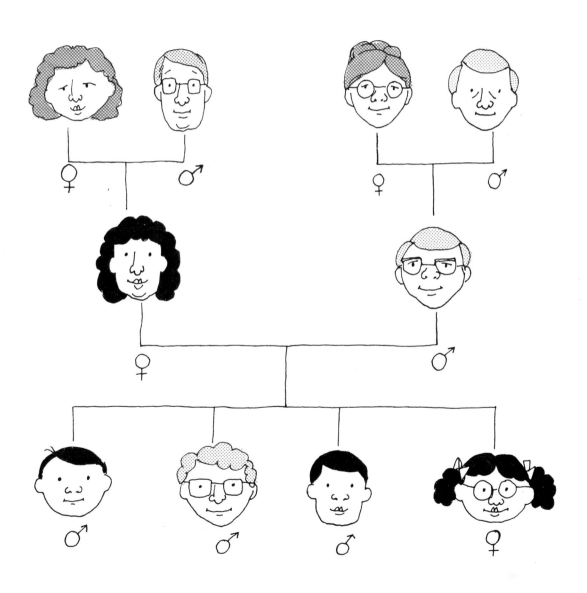

# HIBERNATION OF FROGS

Frogs can be caught outside when the weather is warm. During winter they are in hibernation and it is necessary to purchase them from a scientific supply house. If you buy frogs in winter, you will need to continue housing and feeding the frogs after experimenting until you can release them outside in the spring.

Assemble a semiaquatic aquarium for a frog. One end should be a pool of water with a mud bank tapering up to land on the other end. Place a wire screen over the top of the container to prevent the frog from jumping out.

Observe the activity of the frog in a warm room, the pulsing of its throat as it breathes rapidly. Transfer the aquarium to the cold outside for several hours. It may be placed in front of an open window in winter if the rest of the space around the aquarium can be blocked off. Now observe the frog. Its breathing slows down, it becomes slow and sluggish, and starts to burrow into the mud bank. This is hibernation. Adding ice cubes to the pool in the aquarium and scattering them over the aquarium also will cause hibernation.

---

### DEFINITIONS

**hibernation** — a dormant or resting stage for some animals, usually during winter months

---

# HYDROMETER

A simple hydrometer is an instrument used to determine the density of liquids in relation to the density of water.

Mold a small ball of modeling clay on the end of a thin dowel rod or pencil. Fill a widemouthed jar half full of water. Place the stick, with the clay ball down, into the water. It will sink a certain distance into the liquid. Mark the level on the stick and label it number 1. The distance from the bottom of the clay to the mark is now a unit that represents the density of water. This unit can be used to figure the specific gravity of other liquids.

Repeat the measurement technique above by substituting other fluids for the

water. Figure the specific gravity of cooking oil, molasses, vinegar, and liquid detergent. Determine the distance the stick sinks in each one. Then calculate the ratio between each density with the density of water.

---

### DEFINITIONS

**ratio** — the relationship between two or more things, comparing such factors as size, weight, number, or speed

**specific gravity** — the ratio between equal amounts of two materials, found by comparing their weights. Water is often used as the second substance.

---

## INCUBATOR

Make two wooden or fiberboard boxes, one larger than the other. Cut a small square window in a side of the large box. Cut a slit on top of the small box and suspend an electric bulb with a long cord in the box. Put the small box inside the larger one and pack wall insulation be-

tween them on all sides. Be sure the open end of the small box fits against the side of the large box in which the window was cut. Place a thermometer in the box so you can read it through the window. Fit a sheet of clear plastic or glass over the window.

It is necessary to keep the temperature at 103 degrees Fahrenheit (40 degrees Celsius) both night and day for twenty-one days. Experiment using different bulbs and changing the amount of insulation until the incubator has remained at this temperature for two days. Place a small dish of water in the incubator for moisture. Put a dozen fertile hen's eggs in the incubator. Turn the eggs daily. After the baby chicks hatch, transfer them to a homemade brooder. They should be given mash and fresh water daily.

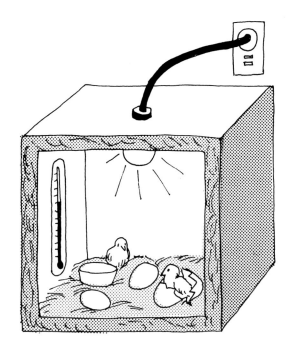

## INSECT COLLECTING

Plan to collect insects in the fall after they have had the opportunity to reproduce during the summer. It is true many insects are harmful to humans and crops and killing them early in the spring would be helpful. However, there are many good and endangered species that should be protected. Since the freezing weather will kill them anyway, one can justify making a collection for study. There are over two hundred insects in the north that migrate south in the fall. You may miss some of these.

In order to capture insects a net must be constructed. Sew a two-foot-long sock of netting to a circle of wire fashioned from a hanger. Bind the ends of the hanger around an old broom handle and tack the wire in place. It is easier to capture insects in the grass than to chase flying ones. Use a sweeping action by swinging the net back and forth so it billows out. Then quickly rotate the wrist, closing off the open end with the insects at the bottom end. Grasp the net to form a closed sack. Pull the netting through your hand until an insect is near. With the other hand reach in and carefully pick up the insect to transfer it to a killing jar. Delicate wings are easily broken with rough handling. Bees, wasps, and other stinging insects should be popped into the killing jar without handling. After a few tries and some lost insects one can become quite skillful at this technique. Insects should be mounted after only one day in the killing jar. If they are too brittle to spread, then they must be put in a relaxing jar.

## INSECT KILLING JAR

A widemouthed peanut butter jar makes a good container for an insect killing jar. Put a layer of cotton soaked in a commercial insecticide in the bottom and cover the cotton with a cardboard or foil disk. This keeps the insects from getting soaked. Leave the insects in the killing jar overnight.

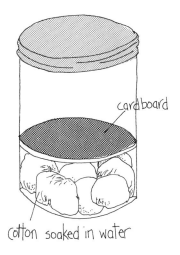
cotton soaked in water

## INSECT RELAXING JAR

There are times you may find an insect that is already dead. Of course, rigor mortis will have set in. There is no way you can spread the wings of butterflies, moths, damselflies, dragonflies, and other insects with delicate large wings without breaking them. It is necessary to design a relaxing jar. It can be made in the same manner as the insect killing jar except the cotton is soaked in water instead of insecticide. When an insect is kept overnight in this high humidity container, you then will be able to mount the insect on a spreading board until it is dry.

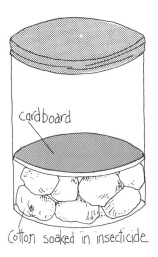
Cotton soaked in insecticide

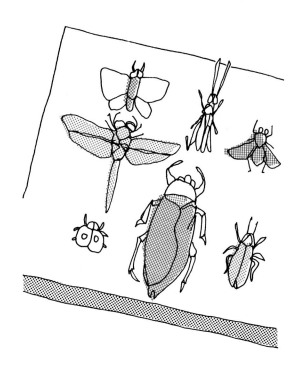

## INSECT SPREADING BOARD

Insects with large membranous wings, such as butterflies and moths, should be pinned on a spreading board in order to dry their wings in an open formation. A spreading board can be made by nailing two stacks of several layers of heavy cardboard to a wooden base, leaving a small groove down the center. The body of the insect lies in the groove and the wings are spread over the cardboard and pinned down with little strips of paper. Do not pin directly into the wings.

## INSECT MOUNTS

Insects can be mounted on pins which are then stuck into the bottom of a cardboard box. A pin should be carefully pushed through the thorax since the abdomen may be too soft to hold the insect in a normal position. The advantage of pin mounting is to permit one to observe the ventral or underside of the animal. Insects may also be placed directly on a cotton layer in a flat box. Cover the box with glass, clear plastic, or tape cellophane over it. A few mothballs should be put under the cotton to prevent other insects from destroying your collection.

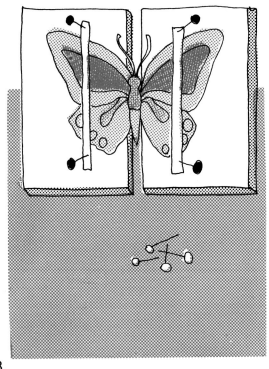

48

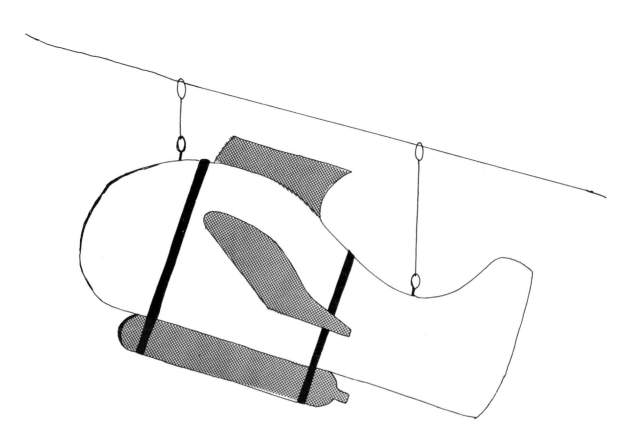

## JET PLANE

Construct a jet plane model out of a block of Styrofoam or balsa wood. Cut out two wings. Finishing nails can be pushed halfway into the inside edges of the wings and the protruding ends into the body of the fuselage. Tape a carbon dioxide cylinder (purchased at a hobby store or science supply house) to the bottom of the plane. Be sure the mouth or front end of the cylinder is pointed toward the tail section. Fasten metal rings or screw eyes to the plane and thread through a long wire. Follow the illustration.

Anchor the wire from one end of a room to the other. You are now ready to blast off. Using a sharp nail or ice pick, puncture the soft metal in the mouth of the cylinder.

Sir Isaac Newton's third law of motion says that for every action there is an equal and opposite reaction. In which direction is the gas escaping in relation to the thrust of your jet plane?

49

## LANTERN SLIDES

Most schools have slide projectors that take 3¼" x 4" or 2" x 2" glass lantern slides. A young artistic scientist can put a wealth of ideas on a set of slides for use in class reports or science fair demonstrations.

Ground glass slides and clear cover glasses can be purchased at most science supply houses. Clear glass will take waterproof india ink, but ground glass is better when drawing with pencils and paints of various colors. The latter permits shading and producing a three-dimensional effect.

A clear glass slide should be taped around the edges over the picture slide. The words or text can by typed or printed on a sheet of cellophane and inserted between the glass slides as an overlay.

There are a number of objects in nature that can be permanently bound between two pieces of glass for projected study. Spore prints, leaf skeletons, dried seaweed, pressed delicate flowers, thin cross sections of stems, feathers, tiny insects, and fish scales and fins are a few natural things that are exciting to view when enlarged by a projector.

# LEAF COLLECTION

Trees are easily identified by the kinds of leaves they bear. Here are several techniques to use in preserving a leaf collection.

Select fresh leaves that have grown to their normal size. Be sure to pick the entire leaf if it is compound in structure. Lay the leaves flat between many layers of newspapers. Place a weight on top of the stack. On the second day replace the papers with dry ones. Most leaves will be dried and pressed in three days. They may be laminated between sheets of clear plastic. Leaves may also be glued on paper. Shellac the entire surface.

For spatter prints place a leaf on a sheet of paper. Hold a piece of fine mesh screening over the leaf. Push a tooth-brush, dipped in tempera paint, back and forth over the screen. Be careful that drops do not form on the underside.

Leaves may be dipped into hot wax for preservation. Hang up each leaf by its petiole or stalk until the paraffin sets.

Place a leaf on blueprint paper. Expose it to the sun for a minute or two. Remove the leaf and immediately dip the paper into a pan of water. Then put it between two paper towels to dry.

Grease the outside of a glass jar. Hold this area over a candle flame until it becomes dark gray. Place a leaf, under-side up, on a stack of papers that will act as a cushion. Roll the smoky area of the jar over the leaf. Then put a white sheet of paper over the leaf. Roll again with a clean jar. The details of the leaf will appear on the paper. This is called a smoke print.

## LEAF PRESS

A botanical press is easy to make. You will need two pieces of wood for the outside. The ends of orange crates are a good size and usually are free for the asking. Nail the centers of two leather straps, or old belts, to the bottom of one of the boards. Place sheets of newspaper and cardboard between the two boards. When a specimen is found, carefully spread it out between the papers. Tie the straps to hold the press tight. A small handle makes the press easy to carry through woods and roadsides. Be sure you know when a leaf is compound (many leaflets to one bud). If you collect just one leaflet, you will be forever and a day trying to identify the tree or shrub.

Since some wild flowers are rapidly disappearing from nature haunts, there are rules about picking them. Know the laws of your state and then pick only those specimens that are numerous. Better yet, identify and diagram the flower in the field and don't pick it.

## LICHENS

Lichens can be collected anywhere from the tundra to the tropical rain forest. A lichen is a combination of two plants living together. The alga provides the food while the fungus anchors the lichen and absorbs water. These pioneers of the soil live on bare rock. They produce acid that slowly breaks the rock into soil. Some species grow on the bark of live and dead woody plants. Branching forms hang in huge masses from trees. The little red-capped British soldiers grow on the ground in poor soil.

Collect lichens at almost any time of the year. Set up a terrarium with a ground covering of one part loam, one part sand, and two parts humus. Add rocks, twigs, and pieces of bark. Keep a lid on the terrarium and place it in a sunny but cool location. Do not overwater or mold will soon appear. Some lichens you collect may look dry and dead. After a few days in the humid terrarium the algae turns greenish and begins to grow. Soon fungal spores begin to grow and life continues.

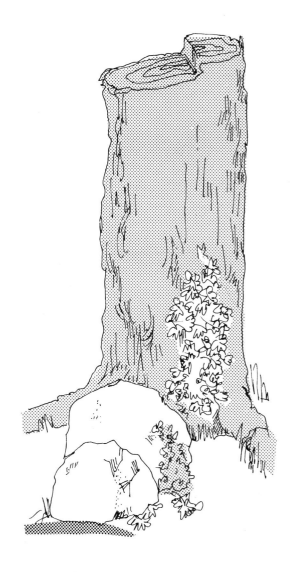

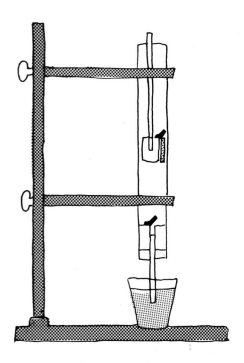

## LIFT PUMP

A lift pump is a type of suction pump used to bring water up out of wells. It can be found on farms and in picnic areas of forest preserves.

Purchase a piece of plastic cylinder or glass chimney about one inch in diameter and a foot long. Build a wooden support or use a ring stand to hold it in a vertical position. Locate a one-hole stopper and a short glass tube to fit into it. Tack a flap of rubber over the top of the hole in the stopper. This arrangement is called the foot valve and should fit snugly in the bottom of the plastic cylinder.

Push a pencil into one hole of the other stopper. Tack a rubber flap over the second hole. This stopper should fit loosely into the top of the plastic cylinder so that when you hold the pencil it will move up and down. It serves as the piston valve.

Place a pan of water under the pump so that the glass tube in the foot valve extends down into it. Prime the pump by pouring a little water in the top of the plastic cylinder. Move the piston up and down. When do the valves or rubber flaps open and close? What happens to the air in the cylinder on the downstroke? What happens when you pull the piston back up?

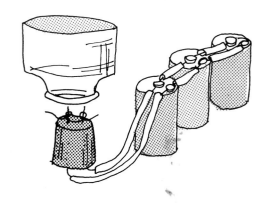

## LIGHT BULB

Push two exposed ends of bell wire through a cork. Wrap fine wire around the end of one wire, then across and around the second wire. This will be the filament in a homemade light bulb. Insert the cork into the mouth of an ink bottle. Connect the other ends of the wire to a series of dry cells. If the circuit is complete the filament will glow. Eventually the filament burns up since there is oxygen in the bottle. This gas has been removed in commercial bulbs.

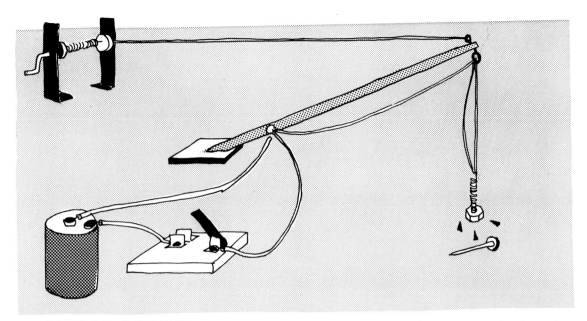

## MAGNETIC CRANE

Construct a cab for the crane out of plywood. Make it similar to those used on most road or house construction jobs. Fasten a miniature windlass (axle and two wheels off a toy car), a dry cell, and a knife switch on the floor of the cab. A projecting arm (dowel rod or 1" x 1" stick) with the lower end sawed at a 45° angle should be fastened by an elbow hinge toward the front of the cab floor. Fasten one eye hook into the top forward end of the projecting arm and another at the lower end. Take several feet of heavy string, anchor one end to the axle of the windlass and the other end to the eye hook at the top of the projecting arm. By turning the handle of the windlass you can raise and lower the projecting arm.

Fasten one end of a piece of bell wire to the outside terminal of the dry cell and the other end to one terminal on the knife switch. Now take several feet of bell wire, fasten one end to the other terminal of the switch, continue through the eye hook at the lower end of the projecting arm, up its length to the forward end, through the second eye hook. Let several inches hang free. Then wrap the wire as a coil around an iron bolt. This will be the electromagnet. Lead the wire back to the top of the projecting arm, through the eye hook, down the arm, and through the lower eye hook. Fasten this remaining end of the bell wire to the middle terminal on the dry cell.

When you turn the windlass arm it will lower the electromagnet to the ground level. Close the knife switch and the magnet will attract any object made of iron or steel. Try picking up objects and transferring them to a container as if you were loading a ship or a boxcar.

55

## MARINE LIFE

A saltwater aquarium will serve as a satisfactory home for live mollusks or shellfish. The tank should have a wide, open top so that a large surface of water is exposed to oxygen in the air. Put two inches of clean sand on the bottom of the tank. Make seawater by following this recipe: four liters of water, three ounces of salt (sodium chloride), a few grains each of potassium sulfate, magnesium chloride, and magnesium sulfate. Pour a few inches of this seawater over the sand.

Root live seaweed, water grass, and Irish moss in the sand. Place a paper over the water and plants while you finish filling the tank. The paper prevents the water from stirring up the sand.

Now the ocean home is ready for inhabitants. If you live along the seashore, mollusks can be captured firsthand. Otherwise one must purchase them from a supply house. Interesting animals to raise are baby octopuses, squid, mussels, snails, limpets, or scallops. Be sure to determine which animals can live together.

## MICE

White mice are gnawers. They need a cage with no exposed wood on the inside. Cover the wooden frame inside with wire mesh. Make the floor of wire screening. Use a shallow pan beneath to catch waste materials. Keep the cage out of direct sunlight and at room temperature.

Fasten food and water containers to the side of the cage to prevent overturning. Feed your mice leafy vegetables, birdseed, and raw potatoes. They must have fresh water daily.

A female mouse may be bred when she is three months old. When she is pregnant, give her milk. She'll also need shredded newspaper to build a nest. Do not disturb the mother after the babies are born. Try not to handle her. If she becomes frightened she might eat her babies. She should not be bred again until the young mice are three to four weeks old and can be weaned. The gestation period for white mice is around twenty days. Litters number between five and fifteen offspring.

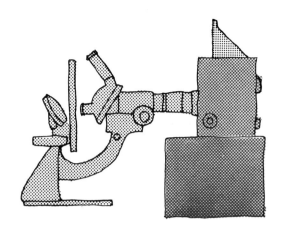

## MICROPHOTOGRAPHY

Many microscopic creatures not seen by the naked eye can be captured on film. Plant cells when magnified are beautiful to study. Live protozoans can be photographed. A helpful hint to slow down the tiny creatures is to put a drop of the culture in a little bit of white syrup. They find it almost impossible to move their organs of motion and will sit still for their picture to be taken.

Make a wet mount of pond water. Place this slide under the objective on the stage of the microscope. Direct as much light as possible upon the specimen to be photographed. Use low or high power depending on the size of the plant or animal. Secure as sharp a focus as possible.

Using electrician's tape, seal the lens opening of the camera directly over the eyepiece of the scope. Set the range finder on infinity. While taking the picture be careful not to jar the instrument.

Microphotography takes patience, experience, and a general knowledge of photography.

---

**DEFINITIONS**

**protozoans** — one-celled animals, usually microscopic, in the phylum Protozoa. Many are aquatic.

---

# MICROSCOPIC SLIDES

From a science supply house purchase plain microscopic slides, cover slips, and a bottle of balsam. The latter chemical will be used to secure a specimen and cover slip to a slide.

For permanent slides select small specimens that are semitransparent. Paper-thin slices of plant and animal tissues can be cut with a homemade microtome or sharp knife. Place the specimen on the center of a slide. Warm the balsam by placing the bottle in a pan of hot water until the material is the consistency of thin syrup. Using a pipette put one drop on top of the tissue. Carefully place the cover glass over it so that no bubbles can form. Tap the glass gently until the balsam spreads out to the edge of the glass. The slide will dry in a couple of days and be ready for observation under a microscope.

---

### DEFINITIONS

**microtome** — an instrument used to slice plant and animal tissues for viewing under a microscope

---

# MICROTOME

A microtome is an instrument used by scientists to cut extremely thin slices of plant or animal tissue. It is used to prepare specimens for microscopic viewing.

A crude homemade microtome can be assembled from a large nut and bolt. Screw the nut onto the bolt one turn only. If you have a flat-headed bolt it will stand upright with the nut on top. Select a specimen like a geranium stem that will stand in the hollow end of the nut. Melt a small amount of paraffin and pour it into the nut around the stem. When the paraffin hardens the stem will be embedded in it and ready for use. Turn the nut clockwise only an eighth of a turn. With a sharp knife or single-edged razor blade cut a thin slice of stem and wax protruding from the end of the nut. Place it on a slide for cellular examination under a microscope. If done carefully one can get a paper-thin section of tissue only one or two cells thick.

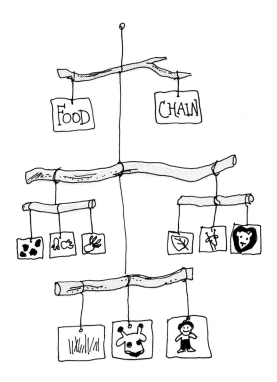

Use drawings or pictures of each link in a food chain. Collect several twigs of different lengths to be used as the cross arms. Tape a short piece of thread at the top center of each picture. Tie the first and third link in the chain to each end of the twig. Locate the absolute center of the twig where it balances and tie the middle link in the chain to this spot. Put a spot of glue on each thread where it is tied to keep it from slipping out of balance. Fasten the first twig to the bottom of a long cord to be used to hang the mobile from the ceiling. Work from the bottom up. When complete, all branches should balance and swing freely.

## MOBILES

Mobiles will brighten up a corner of your world whether it's at home or school. They will test your skill at balancing objects, drawing accurately, and arranging a pictorial story. Science is rich in patterns that involve steps, layers, or sequences of classifying.

Here is one idea—a mobile of a food chain on each branch or swinging arm. A food chain shows who eats what. Examples could be: algae eaten by daphnia that is consumed by a hydra; leaves → deer → lion; seeds → mouse → hawk; and grass → cow → humans.

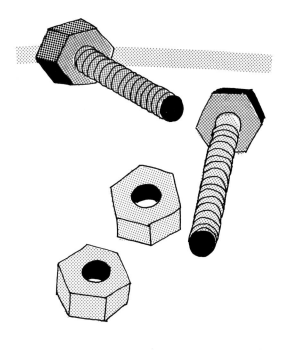

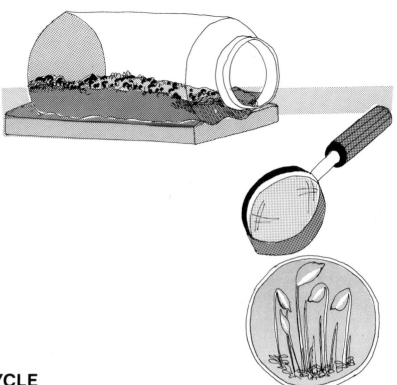

## MOSS CYCLE

Take a hike into the woods to gather moss. It will usually be found in moist, shady places. Transfer the plants and soil to a woodland terrarium. Water well and do not keep your moss house in direct sunlight. A little sulfur sprinkled on the soil will prevent growth of mold.

Examine the tops of the little upright shoots with a hand lens. One kind will produce sperm and another will form eggs. After an egg is fertilized by the sperm, a little stalk grows up out of the female plant. At the top of the stalk will be the capsule containing spores. When the capsule breaks open, the spores fall to the soil and germinate into new plants. The tiny green plants are the sexual generation while the brownish stalk and capsule are the asexual generation.

### DEFINITIONS

**asexual generation** — one of two generations in the life cycle of some plants, in which the spores or reproductive cells grow into plants that produce eggs and sperms

**egg** — the reproductive cell of most female animals and plants; unites with sperm or male cell to produce a new organism

**fertilization** — the joining of an egg and sperm to form a new organism

**sexual generation** — one of two generations in the life cycle of some plants, in which eggs and sperms are produced and the fertilized egg grows into the asexual plant

**sperm** — the reproductive cell of most male animals and plants, that unites with an egg or female cell to produce a new organism

## NATURE CENTER

A nature center is an outdoor science laboratory where students can observe, experiment, record, and learn many new concepts. Often the grounds around a school or your own backyard are uninteresting green deserts, lawns mowed so short that no animals or wild flowers can live there. Take a section of yard or school grounds and turn it into an exciting environmental lab.

Set up a weather station that has these instruments: rain gauge, wind vane, anemometer, hygrometer, thermometer, and snow gauge. A large box on its side can be used for instruments that must be sheltered from the elements.

Near a clump of trees and shrubs build and set out a variety of birdhouses, feeding stations, and a birdbath.

In another corner of your nature center plan a number of garden plots: wild flowers, cultivated plants, herbs, prairie grasses, vegetables, and a tree nursery. Cold frames and a small greenhouse can be constructed out of old storm windows. Flats of seeds can be germinated early in the spring. This is the best way to learn about botany.

Plan a nature trail. Write interesting facts about a number of plants on cards. Glue the cards to pieces of wood and apply two coats of exterior varnish. Nail these on top of stakes that can be driven in the ground next to specimens.

If you still have room left in the laboratory setting, add a compost pile, sundial, small pond, and a few benches where friends can sit and reflect on the out-of-doors.

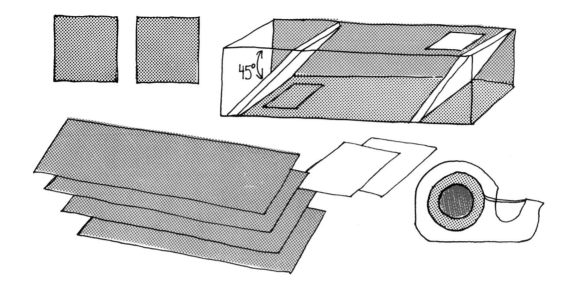

## PERISCOPE

If you are too short to see over people's heads in a crowd, make this periscope. It will also enable you to peek around corners without being noticed.

Cut four strips of balsa wood measuring three inches by one foot. These will form the sides of the tube. Cut two more pieces measuring three by three inches for the ends. Cut out a two-inch square near the end of two side strips. Tape pocket mirrors at a 45° angle to the two sides with holes. Follow the illustration carefully. Tape the remaining sides and the top and bottom pieces to form a completely closed box.

The periscope is now ready for use. Hold the tube upright and look through the bottom opening. Since light travels in straight lines the mirrors will reflect objects down to your eyes.

## PHOTOMETER

A photometer is an instrument that measures the intensity or brightness of light. It compares an unknown source of light with a known one.

Make a groove in a block of wood to hold a piece of white cardboard upright. The cardboard must be white on both sides. Put modeling clay in the groove to help hold it firmly. Drill holes, one on each side of the cardboard and an inch and a half from it, to hold the pencils, lead ends up.

Mounds of clay on separate pieces of wood will hold the three candles. The two candles (double candle) should be very close together so they shine as one. The candles should all be about the same height.

Place the double candle and the single candle about two feet apart with the photometer an equal distance between them. One shadow will be darker than the other. Move the photometer back and forth until the shadows are equally dark. Notice that the photometer is about half as far from the single candle as it is from the double candle.

When the photometer is an equal distance from the light sources and the shadows are equally dark, the sources are equally bright. Test a miniature lamp in a socket. Place it exactly as far from the photometer as the candles are on the other side. Add candles until the shadows are equally dark. You have found the candlepower of the lamp.

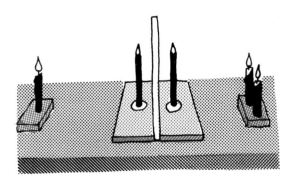

## PLANETARIUM

A planetarium is a machine that projects the night sky on a dome-shaped ceiling. It can portray the positions of the stars, planets, and moons in relation to each other and the sun during the different seasons of the year. A simple planetarium can be made to illustrate a few concepts about astronomy.

Use a large rubber ball and a small ball one fourth its size to represent the earth and the moon. Insert a wire hanger through the center of both balls. Construct a wooden arm on a table lamp by following the adjoining illustration. A large eye screw will permit the arm to revolve around the light, which represents the sun. A spool nailed to the opposite end of the arm will hold the wires attached to the two balls.

When using the planetarium to demonstrate concepts, the axis of the earth should always be tilted to the north as you revolve it around the sun. Use a compass to set the direction correctly. Observe the area on the earth directly illuminated by the light at each quarter turn. Can you figure out which season of the year it is? In what positions will the moon be when there are lunar and solar eclipses?

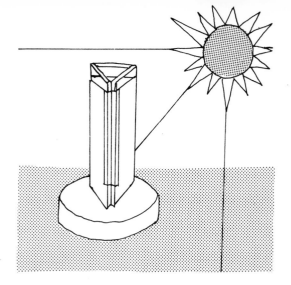

## PRISM

A prism is a solid transparent device that separates white light into the colors of the spectrum: red, orange, yellow, green, blue, and violet. A common type has triangular ends. A homemade prism can be made out of glass and water.

Stand three microscopic glass slides on end with all sides touching to form a triangle. Use narrow strips of clear tape to tape the slides in this position. Pour a little plaster of paris mixture in the lid of a jar. Set the taped slides in the wet plaster and let it dry. Fill the chamber of the prism with water and place it on a windowsill in the sunlight. Can you find a spectrum somewhere in the room that resembles a rainbow?

---

### DEFINITIONS

**spectrum** — the band of color seen when light is separated according to wavelengths. The spectrum of colors from the sun that you can see goes from red (long waves) to violet (short waves).

---

## RADIO

You won't be able to get news from around the world on this homemade crystal radio set. However, it will pick up local broadcasts of sports games or weather reports.

The following items must be purchased at a hardware or radio store: sixty feet of fine enameled wire (number 26 or number 30), a cardboard cylinder, earphone with connections, thirty-five feet of antenna wire and insulator mountings, a germanium crystal diode, tuner strip cut from tin, clips (Fahnstock type), small screws or nails, and a mounting board.

Wrap fifty feet of the wire neatly on the cylinder, providing connecting ends. Fasten the cylinder to the board and position the tuner strip so it will rub along the length of the wire coil. Remove enamel from the wire with sandpaper at points where the tuner rubs. Connect the antenna to the coil and tuner. Attach a ground wire (as from a water pipe) to the other end of the coil and to one side of

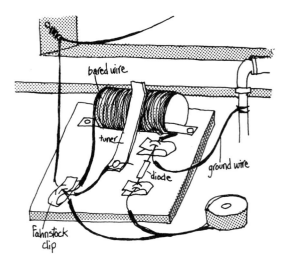

the crystal diode. Follow the illustration carefully. The earphone wires attach to the antenna side and to the diode.

You are ready to tune in once you have checked all connections to be sure they are tight. Rub the tuner back and forth until a powerful radio station in your area can be heard.

## REPTILES

Purchase a healthy turtle from a reliable pet shop, for a sick one can cause illness in humans. Any turtle found outside should be checked by a vet before keeping it as a pet. Either an old aquarium or terrarium can serve as a home. Some require a semiaquatic environment, while others survive in a desert habitat. Study your species and determine the type of soil, plants, and diet needed. A box turtle will eat mealworms and insects, while a tortoise needs vegetables and fruits.

Lizards make interesting pets. Most of them require a desert or woodland habitat. Lizards lick water from plants and the glass sides of a terrarium, so their home requires daily misting. Most reptiles thrive in temperatures from 65 degrees to 80 degrees Fahrenheit. Do not put a lizard terrarium in direct sunlight.

An old aquarium will serve as a comfortable home for nonpoisonous snakes, such as the hognose or garter. They can be found along streams, in woods, or in meadows. They do not like drafts. Wire cages are rough on their skin. Be sure the cover is fastened securely. Stock the house with plants fitting to the species: woodland, desert, or aquatic habitat. Snakes need fresh water daily and raw meat, live insects, grubs, small rodents, or live worms weekly. If a reptile pet fails to eat and behave normally after two weeks in captivity, return it to its natural environment. When handling a snake hold it near the head and in the center of its body. Quick motions and the fear of falling frighten snakes. Leave them alone at feeding time or while they are molting.

## RESPIRATORY MODEL

Find a clear plastic quart or half-gallon jar. Carefully cut the bottom off. Drill a hole in a cork stopper the size of the end of a Y tube. Insert the Y tube into the cork and place a small balloon on each of the two end forks. Place the stopper into the neck of the jar. Be sure that it fits tightly. Secure a cut circle of a heavy balloon over the bottom of the jar with a string. Tape the circle to the jar to prevent it from slipping off. This will serve as the "diaphragm," the large muscle under the lungs that helps you to breathe.

You are ready to illustrate exhalation and inhalation—breathing in and out. Remember there is no muscle tissue in the lungs. They can let air in and out only when the diaphragm and muscles between your ribs (intercostals) contract and relax.

Push up on the "diaphragm." This is its relaxed position. Does the air enter or leave the lungs (balloons)? When the diaphragm is flat it is in a contracted state. What happens to the balloons? What action of the diaphragm muscle helps one to inhale air?

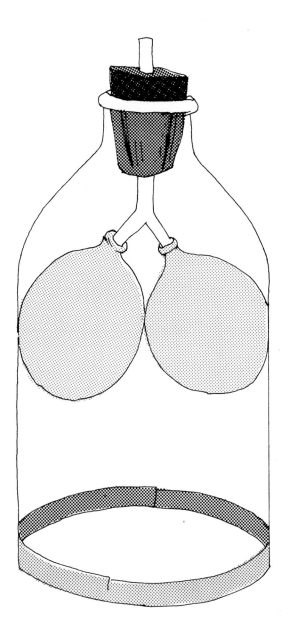

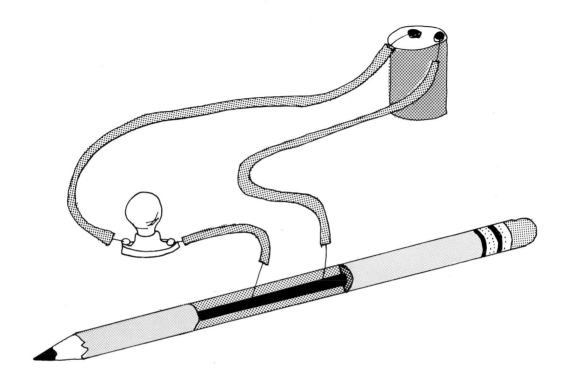

## RHEOSTAT

A rheostat is a device that introduces a resistance into an electric circuit.

A simple rheostat can be made using a lead pencil. Shave away the wood on one side of the pencil to expose the graphite (lead). Since a pencil is usually made of two pieces of wood, it can be split simply by making two cuts down to the lead. Graphite is a poor conductor of electricity.

At a hardware store purchase a small light socket, bulb, bell wire, and a 1½ volt dry cell. Cut three pieces of bell wire and scrape the insulation off the ends.

Follow the adjoining illustration to attach the wire to the socket and dry cell. Hold the free ends of the wire together to make sure the circuit is closed. The bulb should light. Now hold them both on the pencil lead about one eighth of an inch apart. Does the bulb light? Gradually move one wire farther from the other, keeping both pressed tightly to the lead. What happens to the light? By increasing the length of lead in the circuit, you are increasing the resistance. Have you ever been in a home or theater when the lights have dimmed slowly? You may have a rheostat, or dimmer switch, in your home.

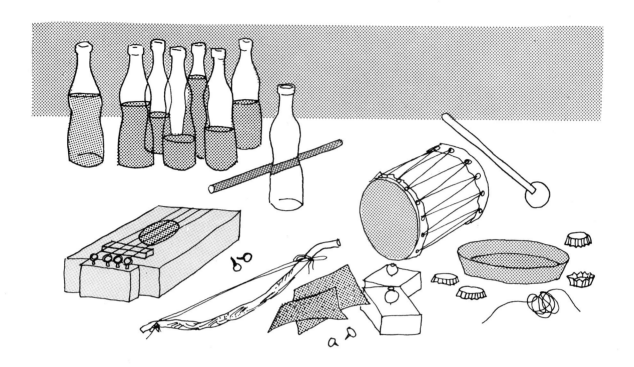

## RHYTHM BAND

Follow these directions for making musical bottles, a violin, drum, tambourine, sand blocks, and chimes. When you have made them, find several friends and make your own music.

Get eight bottles the same weight and size. Leave one empty. Put varying amounts of water in the others so the column of air left in each bottle can be tuned to a note of the musical scale. Use a stick to tap each bottle. Which bottle makes the highest note? The lowest note?

For a violin cut a large hole in the cover of a cigar box. Fasten a strip of wood on one end with screws. Fasten four small eye screws on the top end of this board and on the side of the other end of the box. Attach four pieces of

picture wire across the violin to these screws. They may be turned in order to loosen or tighten the wires while tuning your violin. A small piece of wood should be inserted under the wires near one end of the box. A bow may be made from a curved stick and several long strands of hair.

For a drum remove both ends from a coffee can. Cut circles from a large worn-out beach ball or balloon about two inches larger than the open ends of the drum. With heavy cord or leather thongs lace the circles over the ends of the can. The drum may be hit with the hand or a beater made with a dowel rod inserted into a solid rubber ball.

For tambourines find two old pot covers or wire two bottle caps back to back. Fasten pairs of these to the rim of an aluminum pie pan.

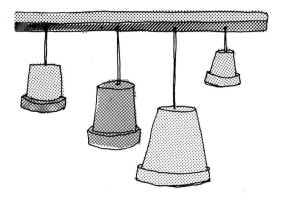

to hold it down. Feed your pet small live insects, mealworms, or earthworms. If it does not consume any food the first few days, return it to its natural environment. Some animals simply will not adjust to a captive life.

For sand blocks tack a strip of sandpaper to wooden blocks. Fashion a handle for the top. Use different coarseness of paper to vary the sounds.

Select a number of clay pots of different diameters. Suspend them in order of size from a wooden support so they hang freely. Use a small wooden mallet to strike them. These will simulate chimes.

## SALAMANDERS

Take a hike along a stream in a damp wooded area to look for salamanders. They appear in the open right after a rainfall. Use gloves to pick them up since some salamanders have poison glands on their skins. Place them in a box containing wet grass and soil to transport them home.

A semiaquatic terrarium is an ideal habitat. This glass house should have a saucer or a cake pan of rainwater at one end and a land habitat elsewhere. Keep a screen over the top with a weight on top

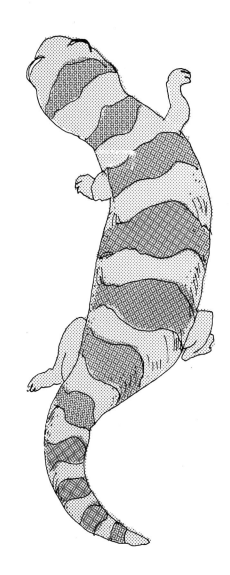

Design a scene and sketch it lightly on the mat with pencil or chalk. It could be a wild flower, butterfly, bird, painted turtle, or a snake if you are a reptile fancier. Work only a small area and one color at a time. With a small brush put glue or rubber cement on a section—for example, the petals of a flower. Sprinkle on the correct colored sand at once. Shake off the excess. Continue with the other parts until the picture is complete. You may want to add a blue sky with white clouds. As you become more expert at the technique you can add a plant or animal in its natural habitat.

Frame your picture out of natural wood. Find four branches or pieces of bark. Cut them slightly longer than the sides of your picture. Notch the branches at the four corners halfway through the diameter of the branch and the width of the branch. This makes a frame that is flush on the back side. Carefully tack your mat to the frame. Study the accompanying illustration.

## SAND PICTURES

If you have a flair for art and science you will enjoy this project. Prepare a heavy mat for a picture from recycled paper. Make a number of colored dyes from parts of plants. Use the dye to color several piles of sand and let the sand dry thoroughly.

| Color | Plant Part |
|-------|-----------|
| yellow | onion skins, pear leaves, tanglewood stems |
| orange | carrot roots, mountain ash berries, osage orange roots |
| gold | goldenrod petals |
| tan | onion skins |
| brown | coffee beans, walnut hulls |
| black | red sumac leaves |
| blue | red maple bark, larkspur petals, blueberries, blackberries, blue ash bark |
| green | spinach, most green leaves |
| purple | pokeweed berries, red cedar roots |
| red | red onion skins, red rapsberries, sumac berries, bloodroot roots, strawberries |

## SKELETON MOUNTS

To obtain skeletons use a freshly killed fish, frog, turtle, chicken, and rodent for representative examples from each class of vertebrates.

First remove the epidermal covering by skinning the animal. Next boil the animal for an hour. Cut, pick, and scrape all muscles and organs from the skeleton. If necessary boil it again to remove any remaining tissue. The bones can be bleached by covering them with a 3 percent solution of hydrogen peroxide for a day. This chemical is sold in drugstores. Use wire, glue, and small screws to reassemble the skeleton into the shape of the animal. Mount it on a wooden base for support and display.

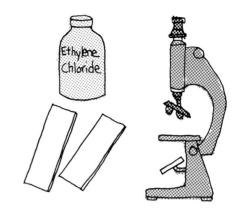

| DEFINITIONS |
| --- |
| **vertebrate** — an animal that has a column of bones down the dorsal side; primitive forms have a notochord or stiff rod |

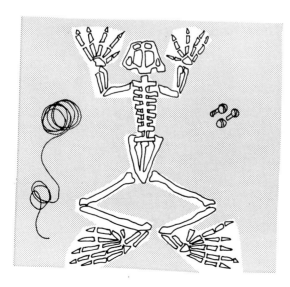

## SNOWFLAKE CASTS

Every snowflake is different. They are beautiful to observe under the microscope in the summer months but must be captured and preserved in the winter.

The compound for this project is a liquid called ethylene chloride. It must be purchased from a science supply house. You also will need clear microscopic slides but no cover glasses.

Pick a calm wintry day when the snow is falling in delicate, fine flakes. The temperature should be around 15 degrees Fahrenheit. Set the slides and solution outside in a protected place until they are cold. A refrigerator also can be used to get them down to the proper temperature.

Expose a slide to the snowfall. When a dozen flakes have hit the slide, quickly put a drop of the solution on each flake. Since this compound is very volatile it will evaporate in minutes, leaving the casts of the snowflakes. When brought indoors the original flakes melt and evaporate from the thin coat of ethylene chloride. Their delicate patterns are permanent.

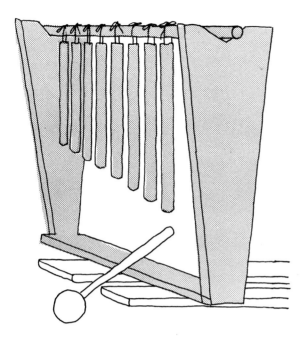

Cut each of the next pieces longer or shorter to make a scale. You may have to file the tubes a little to get the right pitch. Test each pitch by striking the corresponding note on the piano. Drill holes in the ends of the tubes and hang them with string from the horizontal bar. Make a mallet for striking the sound pipes by inserting a dowel into a small, hard rubber ball.

Here is an appropriate scale (in inches) to follow: middle C—$12\frac{7}{8}$, D—$12\frac{1}{4}$, E—$11\frac{1}{2}$, F—$11\frac{1}{8}$, G—$10\frac{21}{32}$, A—$9\frac{31}{32}$, B—$9\frac{3}{8}$, C—9.

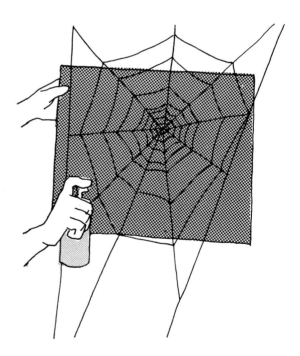

## SOUND PIPES

When a length of pipe is struck a sharp blow, a sound is heard because the air inside the tube has been made to vibrate. The pitch of the sound can be controlled by cutting the pipe to a certain length. This makes the column of air inside vibrate the correct number of times per second.

For example, a piece of pipe exactly $12\frac{7}{8}$ inches long will vibrate at the same frequency or pitch as middle C on the piano. On a series of sound pipes you can play accurate scales and tunes.

First build a wooden V-shaped frame. Over the top put a length of pipe from which the sound pipes will be suspended.

## SPIDER WEBS

Spider webs are found in a variety of places—in the corners of buildings, across strands of tall grass and shrubs, and between rows of corn in a field.

They may be in corners of dark storage rooms and attics.

Carefully place black or dark construction paper on one side of a web until it touches. Gently spray plastic into the web. When it dries, the web will be permanently cemented to the paper.

Collect as many webs as you can find in different patterns and shapes. What kind of spider spun each one? Spinning a web in a particular design is instinctive behavior by the arachnids.

## SPRING SCALE

First you will need a support similar to a commercial ring stand. To make one, fasten with screws an upright 2″ x 2″ board at least 1½ feet high to an eight-inch square base of wood. Place the upright about one inch from one edge of the base. Screw a 2″ x 2″ x 4″ arm to the top of the upright. Follow the illustration. Put an eye hook on the underside at the free end of the arm. You now have a support stand for a variety of experiments. Try this one.

Hang a strong rubber band from the hook. Tie a hook eye at the bottom of the rubber band. Use a hook to suspend a small plastic pail that holds about a cupful of objects. While the pail is hanging, place a line on the upright post to designate the distance the empty pail hangs from the crossbar. Now select a dozen or so objects of the same size, such as large nails, bolts, or nuts, to be used as units of measurements. Put one nail in the pail. Mark a second line on the upright and label it number 1. Continue adding nails, one at a time, and mark the distance the pail drops with each added weight. You should have a series of uniform marks or a scale on the upright usable for weighing objects.

Start by predicting the weight of an object. How many "nails" does a ball weigh? Put it in the pail and weigh it. Did you guess close to its actual weight on your scale? Hold an empty water glass in one hand and pick up nails with the other until you think you have the same weight in both hands. Check it out. Put the glass in the pail and read its weight on the scale.

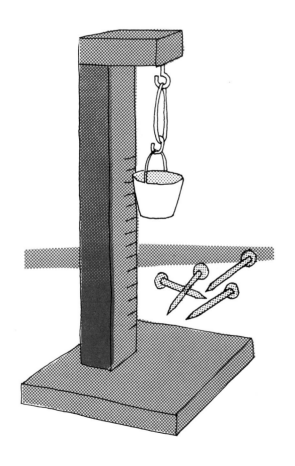

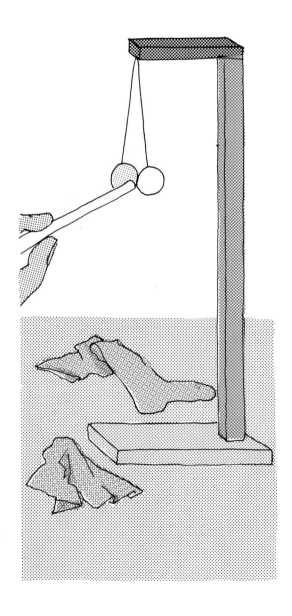

## STATIC ELECTRICITY DETECTOR

Static electricity is produced when two objects or materials are rubbed together. The electrons in the atoms of one will jump to the other. An object becomes positively charged when it gives up electrons. Material that picks up electrons has a negative charge. Set up the following detector and figure out which way the electrons are jumping.

Use two small Styrofoam balls about an inch in diameter. Paint them with a metallic paint. With a long needle, push a thread through the center of each. Knot the thread securely so the balls hang freely, but separately, from a wooden support.

To detect the presence of static electricity, rub a glass rod with a piece of nylon or silk. Hold the rod near the center of the two balls. What happens to them? Now rub a rubber rod with wool and hold it near the balls. Draw conclusions.

---

### DEFINITIONS

**atom** — the smallest particle of matter in all chemical elements

**electron** — a particle of an atom that carries a negative charge and orbits around the nucleus. A flow of electrons produces an electrical current.

## STEAM ENGINE

To assemble a homemade steam engine find a tall, clear, heat-resistant plastic container with a cover. Drill one hole in the bottom of the container and one hole off center in the cover. Cut a circle of plastic from a second cover that will fit into the container. Cut slits in the center of the two covers. Insert a tongue depressor or a pencil in the slits to act as the piston rod. Insert the ends of two pieces of rubber tubing into a cork that fits snugly in the spout of a teakettle.

Boil water in the kettle. Push the other two ends of the tubes slightly into each opening on the ends of the container. Wearing a glove, alternately pinch one tube at a time to shut off the steam. Alternate the steam intake. What happens to the piston rod when you do this? If the exposed end of the piston were attached to a crankshaft, work could be done.

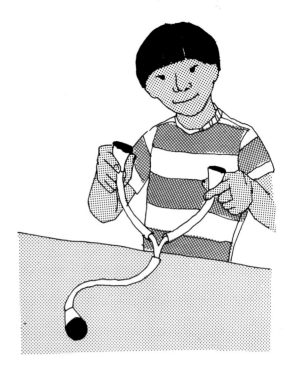

## STETHOSCOPE

A stethoscope is an instrument doctors use to hear your heart beating.

Join the ends of three two-foot pieces of rubber tubing or plastic aquarium hose to the three arms of a glass Y tube. Put small metal funnels on the free ends of the tubing. This will serve as a stethoscope. Have your partner hold two funnels tightly to his ears while you place the third funnel over your heart. If your partner has trouble hearing the beat, put the funnel under your clothes directly on the skin. Count the number of heartbeats per minute. Record. Now run in place for three minutes. Count the heartbeats again. What happens when you exercise strenuously? Continue to listen to the heart. Time how long it takes for it to get back to normal.

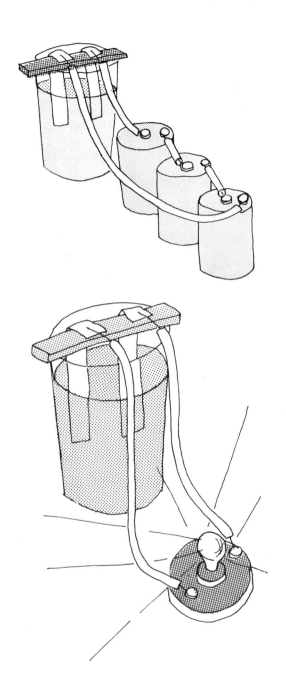

## STORAGE BATTERY

Nail two lead strips to a piece of wood. Attach the exposed ends of two pieces of bell wire to the lead strips. Connect three dry cells in series to the other ends of the bell wire. Set the lead strips in a glass of baking soda solution (one tablespoon of soda to one cup of water). Let this stand for ten minutes. Remove the dry cells from the circuit and substitute a small light. The bulb will glow for several minutes.

Batteries come in all shapes and sizes, but each must contain three necessary parts. These are the anode (active metal strip), the cathode (less active metal strip), and the electrolyte (solution that is a chemical conductor).

For this battery you will need five strips of filter paper that have been soaked in ammonium chloride solution, five strips of zinc, and five strips of copper. Build a stack of materials as follows: a strip of zinc, a piece of wet paper, a strip of copper. Repeat this until all material has been used. End with a piece of metal. Wet the tips of your fingers and put one finger on each end of the stack. Can you feel a slight tingle? This demonstrates the principle of a battery.

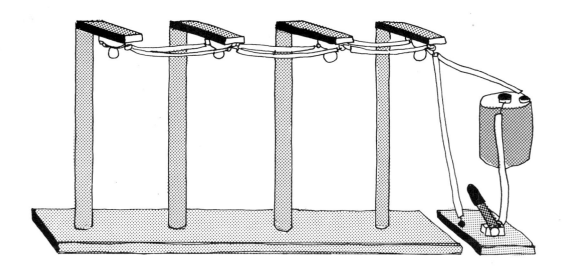

## STREETLIGHTS

The lights lining the streets in your hometown are wired in a parallel circuit. If one goes out the rest of them stay lighted. A mock-up of this system will test your ability as an electrician.

Use pieces of dowel rods for the utility poles. Small scraps of wood nailed to the top of these will serve as the arms that extend out over the street. All poles should be nailed or screwed into a wooden base equal distances apart, or you can drive them into the ground in your yard.

At a hardware store purchase small porcelain sockets, light bulbs, a roll of bell wire, a dry cell (check the volts in relation to bulbs), and a switch.

Screw a light socket under the cross arm at the top of each pole. Cut pieces of bell wire slightly longer than the distance between sockets. Strip the insulation off each end where the wire will be wrapped around the screws on the socket. All wires should run in parallel rows down each side of the lights. Run a wire from one side of the last light to one contact on the switch. Run a second wire from the other contact point to one terminal on the dry cell. Run a third wire from the other terminal back to the other contact point on the last light socket. The circle or circuit is completed. When you push the switch down in a closed position, the street will glow with the model lighting system.

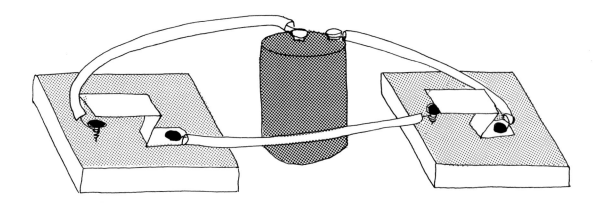

## TELEGRAPH SET

Assemble an electromagnet by wrapping at least twenty turns of bell wire around a screw. Screw the electromagnet into a small board. Cut a strip of metal from a tin can (not aluminum). Make it one inch wide and two inches longer than the length of the screw. This will serve as the armature when fastened near the electromagnet. You have just constructed a telegraph sounder.

Assemble a telegraph key or switch with a second small board, screw, and metal strip. Bend the key upward and

### INTERNATIONAL MORSE CODE

| | | | |
|---|---|---|---|
| A • — | N — • | 1 • — — — — | 6 — • • • • |
| B — • • • | O — — — | 2 • • — — — | 7 — — • • • |
| C — • — • | P • — — • | 3 • • • — — | 8 — — — • • |
| D — • • | Q — — • — | 4 • • • • — | 9 — — — — • |
| E • | R • — • | 5 • • • • • | 0 — — — — — |
| F • • — • | S • • • | | |
| G — — • | T — | | |
| H • • • • | U • • — | Period • — • — • — | |
| I • • | V • • • — | Comma — — • • — — | |
| J • — — — | W • — — | SOS • • • — — — • • • | |
| K — • — | X — • • — | Start — • — | |
| L • — • • | Y — • — — | End of message • — • — • | |
| M — — | Z — — • • | Error • • • • • • • • | |

78

forward as you did for the sounder until the end is just above a screw in the board. The two free ends of bell wire leading from the telegraph sounder should be connected to the screw on the switch and to one terminal on the dry cell. A third wire connects the other terminal to the screw holding the key. Learn the Morse code from the table on page 78 and with a friend send messages back and forth.

## TELEPHONE

Punch a small hole in the bottom of two tin cans. Thread string through each hole and tie it to a button on the inside of the can's bottom. The button will anchor the string so that it won't pull out when pulled tight. Give a friend one can while you hold the other. The string should be long enough so that you can get far apart—too far to talk to each other in normal voices. Stretch the string tight and, while you talk into one can, have your friend hold the other to his ear. Does it become harder to hear each other when the string is allowed to hang loose? Why?

A tin-can telephone shows the way in which sound travels. A real telephone sends sound over wires by changing sound vibrations into electrical impulses inside the telephone mouthpiece or transmitter. The telephone receiver changes the electrical impulses it receives back into sound vibrations.

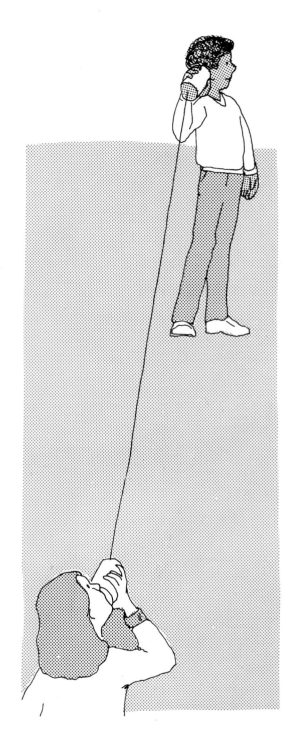

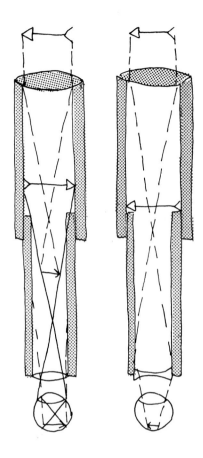

Tape the eyepiece in one end of the smaller tube. Tape the objective lens in one end of the larger tube. Place the small tube inside the larger one. As you look through the eyepiece point the homemade telescope at an object in the night sky. Move the smaller tube in and out until the object is clear. Can you see the moon, Venus, and stars better with this instrument than with the naked eye?

This telescope can be used in the classroom or backyard to magnify things. What happens to the image? Substitute a concave lens for the convex eyepiece. Is your world right side up now?

## TELESCOPE

A refracting telescope is an astronomer's tool used to magnify distant objects. It is based on the principle that light waves are bent or refracted when they pass through different materials.

Locate two cardboard tubes, one slightly smaller in diameter. From a science supply house purchase two convex lenses which have the same or slightly smaller diameters. A suggested focal length for the eyepiece lens is one inch and for the objective lens ten inches. Using lenses of these focal lengths will give you a magnification of ten times.

## TERRARIUMS

Get a large, square, metal cake pan the size you want your finished terrarium to be. If the metal is not aluminum, paint it with aluminum paint. You will have to have glass especially cut for the four sides. (Sheets of clear plastic would be even better.) The sides should be about ten inches high. Their lengths should be slightly smaller than the inside measurements of the cake pan.

Lay the four sides out flat lengthwise on a table. Tape the three joints with strong waterproof tape. Tape the sharp top edges also to keep from being cut. Mix plaster of paris to the consistency of pudding and half fill the cake pan. Let it start to harden, then fold the glass pieces into a rectangle and stand it in the pan. Push down one-half inch into the plaster. Tape the fourth corner. When the

Woodland terrarium

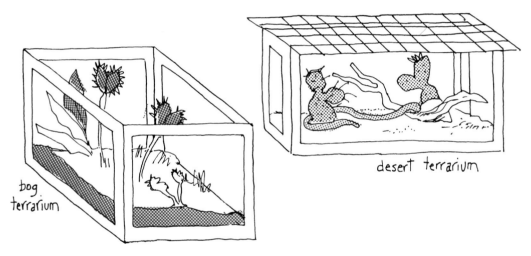

bog terrarium

desert terrarium

semiaquatic terrarium

plaster is dry your terrarium is ready to use.

A glass jar or old aquarium can be used to hold different earth scenes. Be sure to put a glass or wire screen on top of any terrarium that contains animals. Provide the food necessary for each species of animal.

## WOODLAND TERRARIUM

To make a woodland terrarium, spread a layer of gravel and bits of charcoal on the bottom. Cover this layer with several inches of rich garden soil. Small woodland plants, such as wild strawberry, fern, and moss, can be transplanted into it. Salamanders, toads, and tree frogs enjoy this kind of world. Do not put the terrarium in direct sunlight, for these plants and animals prefer shady places.

## DESERT TERRARIUM

A desert terrarium needs sandy soil in which cacti and succulent plants are grown. Small snakes and horned toads thrive in this environment. A desert terrarium can use more sunlight than other kinds.

## BOG TERRARIUM

The bottom of a bog terrarium should contain a mixture of one part sand, one part peat moss, and one part gravel. Bog life prefers more moisture than do other forms of life. This habitat is ideal for insectivorous plants, such as the pitcher plant, sundew, and Venus's-flytrap.

## SEMIAQUATIC TERRARIUM

The scene in this terrarium is a replica of the environment along a riverbank. Place a pan at one end of the container to hold water; the remaining section should be built up with rich soil. Small plants found on the edge of a stream can be grown. Aquatic bladderwort thrives in this world. Tadpoles and water insects can be kept in the water habitat.

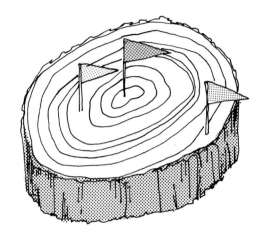

# TREE GROWTH

Secure a cross section of a tree that has been cut down. The slab should be at least five inches thick to prevent the wood from cracking. Sand the surface until it is very smooth. Brush on clear shellac or varnish to bring out the grain in the wood. Starting from the center (the first year's growth) count a light and dark band as one year. Notice how some bands are wider than others. The climate and seasons will affect the width of the rings. What years might indicate a drought? Check with weather records to see if you were right. If your cross section has wider rings on one side than on the other, can you figure out how this happened? How old was the tree when you were born? When you started to school? Place little flags on the annual rings that grew the same year famous historical events happened.

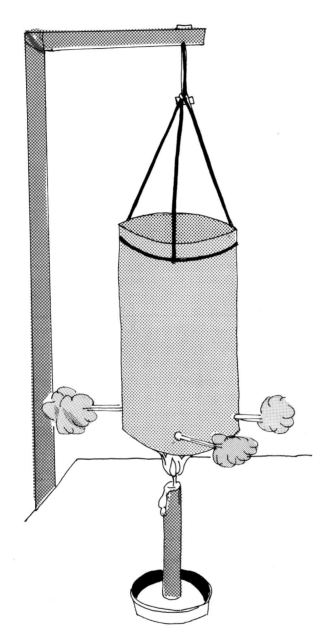

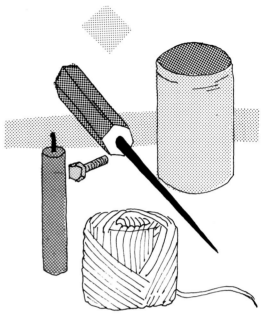

## TURBINE

For a simple turbine, collect a baking powder can with lid, a wooden stand, a candle, string, and ice pick. The lid of the baking powder can must fit tightly. With an ice pick punch three holes approximately one-half inch from the bottom on different sides of the can. Tie a string lightly around the top of the can and fasten three strings from it to a washer and nut and bolt in the top of a stand. The can must be able to swing or rotate freely.

Put a small amount of water in the can—not enough to reach the holes—and put on the lid. As you heat the water over the candle, steam will escape from the holes. What happens to the can?

83

# VEGETABLE GARDEN

Growing a garden presents one with scientific concepts relating to life cycles, pollination, soil nutrients, ecosystems, and conservation.

Select a site that has full sunlight most of the day and crumbly soil with good drainage. Since vegetables require a lot of plant food, test the soil for nitrogen, phosphorus, and potash. Natural fertilizer, such as humus from a compost pile or manure from a farm, is the best to use. Work the fertilizer into the soil to a depth of at least six inches. This will give the roots a loose, aerated mixture in which to grow.

A great deal of planning is necessary before you begin. Measure the area and graph the garden on paper. Purchase seeds that grow well in your climate. An early spring garden can include leaf lettuce, radishes, early peas, onions, green beans, and broccoli. For a summer and fall harvest plant beets, sweet corn, tomatoes, carrots, potatoes, cucumbers, and melons. Read the packages for directions on how deep to plant seeds, the distance between seeds, and the width of the rows or hills.

Throughout the growing season there are always chores to do. Keep the weeds or wild plants pulled. They sap the water and minerals away from the vegetables. Your garden needs to be watered if rains are infrequent. This is especially important during the flowering, fruiting, and root-storing stages. Many vegetables are 70 to 90 percent water.

If your harvest is plentiful a number of vegetables can be stored for weeks or months. Keep potatoes and winter squash in a dark cool place. Tie onions in bunches by the dried leaves and hang them in the garage. Bury carrots in a pail of damp sand. Do not wash vegetables for storage. Try to avoid using any biocides on garden vegetables. Share your harvest with other animals—rabbits, birds, gophers, and insects.

# WATER PURIFICATION

As the human population increases most towns and cities must obtain drinking water from surface bodies rather than from deep wells fed by underground springs. Raw lake and river waters are exposed to pollutants and must pass through a complicated series of steps to be purified for drinking.

A simplified model of the steps in a purification plant can be set up if you follow the diagram.

Locate four clear plastic bottles and one-holed stoppers to fit into the tops. Drill the same size hole near the bottom in the first and third bottles and near the top in the second one. In the latter water is always pulled off above the sediment that filters down in the settling basin. Use rubber tubing inserted in the stoppers on the side of the bottles to lead to the top stopper of the next bottle. Melted paraffin around the holes and stoppers will keep the water from leaking out. The third bottle should be three-fourths full of graded gravel and sand with the coarse material on the bottom. The fourth bottle will hold the purified water. Pinch clamps on the rubber tubing will control the water flow.

Various chemicals are added in the purifying process. Alum clumps with dirt, algae, and other particles so they will settle out. Carbon helps to remove the fishy odor and sour taste from decomposing life in the raw water. Chlorine is added to kill bacteria. Fluorine is helpful in preventing tooth decay.

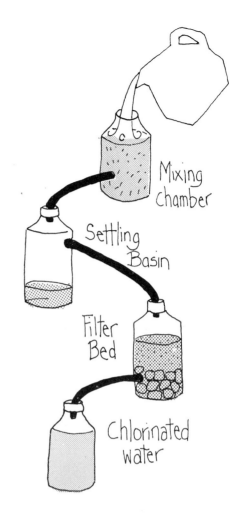

You are now ready to test the purification of water. Get a pitcher of water from a stream that looks dirty and contains algae, the green scum floating on the surface. Pour it into the mixing chamber with a tablespoon of alum and powdered charcoal. Household bleach can be used as a substitute for pure chlorine. NOTE: The finished water will look clean but certainly is *not* purified enough to drink. Only in purification plants, where scientists are trained to control the correct amounts of chemicals, can water be made safe to drink.

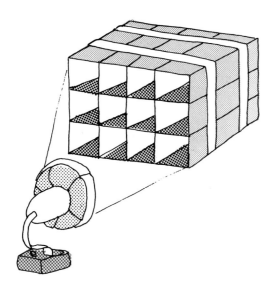

## WIND TUNNEL

A wind tunnel is used by scientists to test model airplanes designed like actual planes. It provides them with information about how a certain plane would respond in flight.

Take a dozen one-quart cardboard milk cartons and cut off both ends on each. Glue all twelve together as shown in the illustration. An electric fan set in front of the wind tunnel will produce the air currents. Model airplanes of balsa wood, heavy cardboard, or plastic can be tested. Hold a plane on the end of a string behind the wind tunnel. Refer to the diagram for position. Does the wind current create a lift? Adjust the elevators on the tail assembly so the airplane will climb. What is the position of the elevators in a nose dive?

## WINDLASS

A windlass is a simple machine, a wheel and axle, used to lift heavy objects. It takes less force to turn the wheel than the force applied to the axle.

Set up a windlass by following the accompanying diagram. Balance a broom handle or dowel rod across the back of two chairs. This will be the axle. Use a tack to anchor each cord to the axle. Weigh an object before you tie it to the end of one cord, the axle. Fasten a spring scale to the other cord, the wheel arm. Turn the wheel arm by pulling the spring scale. How much force did it take? Compare this to the weight of the object being lifted.

Now anchor a salt box to the axle. Fasten the cord with the scale attached to this box. Pull the spring scale and record the weight of the object. What have you gained? Can you figure out what you lost?

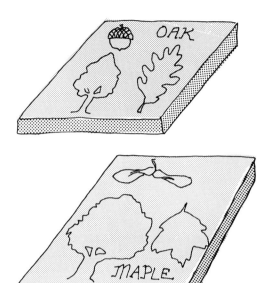

## WOOD SPECIMENS

An interesting and attractive display of varieties of woods can be put together with simple materials. The people at a lumberyard or sawmill will be helpful in furnishing scraps of various hard and soft woods. Be certain each wood is properly identified before you begin.

Cut the scraps into uniform sizes. Sand one surface carefully to make it smooth and to bring out the grain or annual rings. Use a black pencil to outline the tree's shape, leaf shape, fruit, and average height on the wood sample. You may want to add a tree's location or habitat. Apply oil or paste wax on the finished surface. Mount the samples on plywood for display.

## WORMERY

Fill a clear plastic bottle or old aquarium with alternate layers of garden soil, leaf mold, and sand. Sprinkle each layer with a little water. On the top of the last layer place small pieces of leafy vegetables and a handful of cornmeal or oatmeal. Dig up several earthworms from the yard and transfer them to their new home. Cover the jar for a week to encourage the worms to tunnel near the sides.

As the earthworms consume the decayed vegetation, they will keep turning the soil. Feed them twice a week. The worms will reproduce and furnish a ready supply of food for pet amphibians and reptiles.

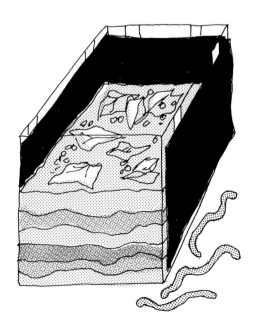

wire screen to prevent larger animals from getting the food. Tie a cord around the bottle and lower it into the water. Fasten the other end of the cord to a stake driven in the ground on the edge of the bank. It will take several hours for the planaria to find the liver. Check periodically for signs of a capture. Transfer the planaria to a glass bowl or jar of fresh water for their future home. Include a few aquatic plants. Once a week transfer them to a shallow feeding dish. Give them small pieces of raw liver or fresh hamburger. Give them a couple of hours to eat before transferring them back to their clean bowl of water.

Earthworms are found in garden soil that is rich in humus and decaying plant and animal material. Turning over spadefuls of soil will uncover these segmented annelids. Fishermen call them night crawlers and use a flashlight at night to locate them on the surface of the damp ground. After a heavy rain they come to the surface in order to avoid drowning. Transfer the animals to a wormery.

Flat, round, and segmented worms can be collected along the shores of oceans. Look for them under rocks, burrowing in the sand, or clinging to aquatic plants. Their habitat must mimic their natural environment.

## WORMS

Planaria are little dark flatworms whose eyespots appear crossed. They are often collected for use in regeneration experiments. Planaria can be found in quiet streams and collected in the following way.

Put a piece of raw liver in a tall olive bottle. Cover the bottle's mouth with a

---

### DEFINITIONS

**regeneration** — the growing on or replacement of a missing body part, or the reproducing of a whole body from one small piece of the original organism

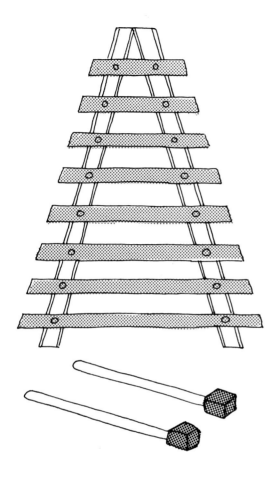

## XYLOPHONE

Most xylophones have three or more octaves, but a simple eight-note model can be built easily. Using clear pine about ½ to ¾ inches thick, cut a sounding bar about 1¼ inches wide and 5 inches long. Be certain to cut sounding bars so the grain runs parallel to the length of the bar. Hold this first bar lightly between two fingers and tap it with another piece of wood to determine what note on a piano you have produced. Cut another piece about 4½ inches long. By tapping both pieces and checking with a piano, see if they are consecutive or nearly consecutive notes. Remember, the shorter the sounding bar, the higher the tone.

If your second bar is too much like the first, saw off what you think may produce the desired tone. Thus, by trial and error, cut eight sounding bars, four longer and three shorter than the first. Sand each so it will be smooth and free of splinters.

Now cut two narrow pieces of wood about 14 inches long and ½ inch square. Next, cut felt strips as long and about as wide as these mounting pieces for the sounding bars. Glue the felt strips to the mounting pieces. Set the mounting pieces in a wide "V" and place the sounding bars along the felted side with a space of about ¼ inch between each bar.

Make a final check to see that you are satisfied with your scale. If you are, drill holes in the bars where they meet the mounting pieces. The holes should be just slightly larger than the nails you intend to use. Be certain the nails have heads large enough to prevent the bars from falling off the mounting pieces when the instrument is being carried. Also be careful that the nails are not so heavy that they split the mounting pieces.

Now all you need is a mallet or two. Drill a hole just large enough to hold a dowel pin handle in the center of a block of wood about 1 inch long and ¾ inch wide. Glue the handles in place. When they have dried you are ready to play.

# Index

**airplane, jet,** making model, 49
**airplane,** making wind tunnel, 86
**alcohol burner,** making, 18
**animal houses,** making, 9, 12, 40, 56, 65
**animal tracks,** making castings, 10
**ant colony,** making, 10
**aquarium,** frog hibernation, 44
**aquarium,** raising guppies, 40
**aquarium, saltwater,** 56
**aquarium projection,** 11
**arachnids,** making cage for, 12
**asexual reproduction,** ferns, 35
**astronomy,** simple planetarium, 63
**atomic structure,** making element models, 32

**balance scale,** making, 12
**ball bearings,** reducing friction, 13
**battery, storage,** making, 76
**belt-driven machines,** spool models, 14
**birdhouses,** making, 14
**blood circulation, animal's heart,** 41
**blood circulation, demonstrating,** 23
**blueprint paper,** making, 16
**bog terrarium,** making, 80
**bone and muscle model,** making, 16
**botanical press,** making, 52
**bottles,** musical, 68
**breathing,** respiratory model, 66
**brooder,** making, 21
**burner, alcohol,** making, 18
**butterflies,** studying, 19

**cages,** for animals, making, 9, 12, 40, 56
**camera,** making, 18
**candlepower,** determining, 62
**caterpillars,** studying, 19
**cell models,** making, 20
**charts,** making, 20
**chicken brooder,** making, 21
**chicken-egg incubator,** making, 45
**chimes,** making, 68
**chromatography,** using, 22
**circulation, blood,** animal's heart, 41
**circulation, blood,** demonstrating, 23
**collection net,** for insects, 46
**compass,** directional, using, 24
**complex machines,** 26
**compost pile,** making, 25

# Index

**compound machines,** 26
**crane,** electromagnetic, model, 55
**crystal radio set,** making, 64

**daphnia,** aquarium projection, 11
**desert terrarium,** making, 80
**diazo paper,** making prints, 27
**dimmer switch,** making, 67
**drum,** making, 68

**earthworms,** making a wormery, 87
**earthworms,** raising, 88
**eclipse viewer,** making, 28
**egg incubator,** making, 45
**electrical charge,** determining, 31
**electrical switch,** making, 30
**electricity,** making galvanometer, 38
**electricity,** making rheostat, 67
**electricity,** making storage battery, 76
**electricity,** static, detecting, 74
**electricity,** streetlight system, 77
**electric quiz game,** 28
**electromagnet,** for crane, 55
**electromagnet,** for telegraph set, 78
**electromagnet,** making, 30
**electroscope,** making, 31
**elements,** making models, 32
**embedding plastic,** using, 34
**embryology,** making cell models, 20

**family traits,** determining, 42
**ferns,** observing life cycle, 35
**flowers, diagraming parts,** 36
**flowers, embedding in plastic,** 34
**flowers, preserving,** 37
**footprints,** animal, making castings, 10
**friction,** using ball bearings, 13
**frogs,** hibernation, 44

**galvanometer,** making, 38
**game,** electric quiz board, 28
**gardening, compost pile,** making, 25
**gardening, grafting plants,** 38
**gardening, greenhouse,** making, 39
**gardening, growing herbs,** 42
**gardening, vegetable garden,** making, 84
**grafting plants,** 38
**greenhouse,** making, 39
**guinea pigs,** raising, 40
**guppies,** raising, 40

**heart, animal's,** blood circulation, 41
**heart,** making a stethoscope, 75

**herbs,** growing, 42
**heredity,** family traits, 42
**hibernation,** of frogs, 44
**hydra,** aquarium projection, 11
**hydrometer,** making, 44

**incubator,** making, 45
**insects, collecting,** 46
**insects, embedding in plastic,** 34
**insects, killing jar,** 47
**insects, making cages,** 9, 12
**insects, mounting,** 48
**insects, relaxing jar,** 47
**insects, spreading board,** 48

**jet plane,** making model, 49

**killing jar,** for insects, 47
**knife switch,** making, 30

**lantern slides,** for projecting, 50
**leaves, collecting,** 51
**leaves, preserving,** 51
**leaves, press,** making, 52
**lichens,** collecting, 53
**lift pump,** making, 54
**light,** making a prism, 64
**light,** measuring brightness, 62
**light bulbs,** making, 54
**liquids,** determining specific gravity, 44
**lizards,** raising, 65
**lungs,** respiratory model, 66

**machines, belt-driven,** spool models, 14
**machines, compound,** 26
**magnet, making electromagnet,** 30
**magnet, making galvanometer,** 38
**magnetic crane,** making, 55
**marbles,** used as ball bearings, 13
**marine aquarium,** saltwater, 56
**mice,** raising in cage, 56
**microphotography,** studying, 57
**microscopes, making microtome,** 58
**microscopes, preparing slides,** 58
**microtome,** making, 58
**mobiles,** making, 59
**moss,** growing, 60
**moths,** studying, 19
**mounts, for animal skeletons,** 71
**mounts, for insects,** 48
**muscle and bone model,** making, 16
**musical instruments,** making, 68, 89
**musical instruments,** sound pipes, 72

# Index

**nature center,** making, 61

**outdoor science lab,** making, 61
**Ozalid paper,** making prints, 27

**paper, blueprint,** making, 16
**paper, diazo,** making prints, 27
**parallel circuit lights,** 77
**periscope,** making, 62
**photography, camera,** making, 18
**photography, microphotography,** 57
**photometer,** making, 62
**pictures,** made of sand, 70
**pipes, sound,** making, 72
**planaria, aquarium projection,** 11
**planaria, raising,** 88
**plane, jet,** making model, 49
**plane,** making wind tunnel, 86
**planetarium,** making, 63
**plants, grafting,** 38
**plants, greenhouse,** making, 39
**plastic, embedding,** using, 34
**press, botanical,** making, 52
**prism,** making, 64
**pump, lift,** making, 54
**purification,** of water, 85

**quiz game,** electric, 28

**radio,** making crystal set, 64
**refracting telescope,** making, 80
**relaxing jar,** for insects, 47
**reptile house,** making, 9
**reptiles,** raising, 65
**respiratory,** model of lungs, 66
**rheostat,** making, 67
**rhythm band,** 68

**salamanders,** raising, 69
**saltwater aquarium,** making, 56
**sand blocks,** making, 68
**sand pictures,** making, 70
**scale, balance,** 12
**scale, spring,** 73
**semiaquatic terrarium,** 82
**sexual reproduction,** ferns, 35
**skeletons, mounting,** 71
**slides, lantern,** for projecting, 50
**slides, microscopic,** preparing, 58
**smoke prints,** making, 51

**snake house,** making, 9
**snakes,** raising, 65
**snowflakes,** making casts, 71
**solar eclipse viewer,** making, 28
**sound pipes,** making, 72
**spatter prints,** making, 51
**specific gravity,** determining, 44
**spiders, collecting webs,** 72
**spiders, making cage for,** 12
**spreading board,** for insects, 48
**spring scale,** making, 73
**static electricity,** detecting, 74
**steam engine,** making, 75
**steam turbine,** making, 83
**stethoscope,** making, 75
**storage battery,** making, 76
**streetlights,** mock-up system, 77
**switch, electrical,** making, 30

**tambourine,** making, 68
**telegraph set,** making, 78
**telephone, tin-can,** making, 79
**telescope, refracting,** making, 80
**terrariums, collecting lichens,** 53
**terrariums, fern life cycles,** 35
**terrariums, growing moss,** 60
**terrariums, making,** 80
**terrariums, raising salamanders,** 69
**tin-can telephone,** making, 79
**tools,** complex, 26
**tracks, animal,** making castings, 10
**trees,** determining age from rings, 82
**turbine,** making, 83
**turtles,** raising, 65

**vegetable garden, growing herbs,** 42
**vegetable garden, making,** 84
**violin,** making, 68

**water,** purification, 85
**water cell,** projecting, 11
**webs, spiders',** collecting, 72
**windlass,** making, 86
**wind tunnel,** making, 86
**wood,** displaying specimens, 87
**woodland terrarium,** making, 80
**wormery,** making, 87
**worms,** making a wormery, 87
**worms,** raising, 88

**xylophone,** making, 89

# ABOUT THE AUTHOR

Helen J. Challand earned her M.A. and Ph.D. from Northwestern University. She currently is Chair of the Science Department at National College of Education and Coordinator of Undergraduate Studies for the college's West Suburban Campus. *Science Projects and Activities* is the fourth book in Dr. Challand's science series. Her other titles are: *Activities in the Earth Sciences*, *Activities in the Physical Sciences*, and *Activities in the Life Sciences*.

An experienced classroom teacher and science consultant, Dr. Challand has worked on science projects for Scott, Foresman and Company, Rand McNally Publishers, Harper-Row Publishers, Encyclopaedia Britannica Films, Coronet Films, and Journal Films. She is associate editor for the *Young People's Science Encyclopedia* published by Childrens Press.